BUSINESS RISK MANAGEMENT

Prof. Kelly M Kingsley

IEM PRESS

PO Box 831001, Richardson, TX 75080

A Subsidiary of IEM APPROACH

ISBN 13: 978-1-947662-86-5

Library of Congress Catalog Card Number: 2020908539

TABLE OF CONTENTS

ACKNOWLEDGEMENT

I am overwhelmed in all humbleness and gratefulness to all those who have helped me to put these ideas into words; it would never have been possible without your support. Special thanks go to Mr. Ediage and Eric Mesumbe for their devotion to the research and data collection, the Mua's family and the Kellys, in particular, for their understanding, love, and support throughout this period. Most importantly, thanks go to Almighty God, Who knew from the beginning that a day like this would happen.

PRELUDE

It is my belief that businesses with a spiritual foundation go farther faster. And I further state that faith and finance can peacefully coexist. I am clear that my Incredible Factor includes my personal relationship with God. Internal control mechanisms, business processes, artificial intelligence, and information and communication technology tools remain key in performance, control, and oversight, but the belief system is like the mortar that holds these together. Over fifty-four Bible verses are clear on the principle on which businesses should be managed, as well as their top-to-bottom, bottom-up, and vertical relationships. The Quran, The Vedas and other religious sacred texts, have these principles as a common denominator because no business can prosper if its governance challenges are not addressed. With over twelve chapters, this piece of work attempts to educate and share findings on topical issues that can improve management in corporate organizations. Governance challenges are also in ministerial departments and agencies; these principles are of equal importance and apply adequately.

Corruption is something we talk about, something we complain about, something whose negative impact we recognize, but the irony and tragedy at once is that those who practice corruption love it, while those who do not practice corruption accommodate it. How can we attain our full potential scientifically, educationally, socially, culturally and so on, with this attitude?

Venality and racketeering are the consequences of the breakdown in moral standards and value. In the world of today, the side we choose, if powerful, defines what is good and what is bad; right and wrong is no longer prescribed by the Good Book, even though the consequences of these bad decisions are multiple, varied, and highly visible. A better world is a function of joint efforts, not of finger-pointing, because we have all failed in nursing, nurturing, and building a productive community. Let us take responsibility for the breakdown in moral standards as we aspire to build strong corporate organizations that will be key in nation-building. A better and stronger world is a function of the reduction of corporate decadence.

INTRODUCTION

This book is the result of a one-year research project on the views of corruption in corporate organizations and government institutions. In post-colonial Africa, we seek to explore the cold war and the rise of dictators with support from the East and West, the decline of democracy and the rise of tyranny and tribal and religious conflicts, Neocolonialism, and using financial institutions to meddle in a country's domestic policies. In Cameroon and Nigeria, the vast corruption in corporate organizations (government companies) and the awarding of government contracts to the custom sector are leading to the enormous cost of doing business, tax evasion, a corrupt insurance sector leading in insecurities in investments, a corrupt judiciary, police, and army, the theft of funds for state arms and machinery, daily police bribery, an unreliable justice system, and the vulnerability of the poor. The way forward seeks to propose the promotion of pan-Africanism as a tool to eliminate religious and tribal conflicts, promote re-orientation to pre-colonial ethical norms and values, and to promote political goodwill and dedication to the country, strengthening anti-corruption watchdogs to facilitate the prosecution of embezzlers and the corrupt.

Regarding international efforts, nations like Switzerland should change laws and make it difficult to attract money-laundering and tax evasion. The nations of Nigeria and Cameroon should draw lessons from the western world, especially the USA and Finland, such as free access to education for all, freedom of speech and the press, independent arms of the government, political goodwill and dedication of service, access to law and justice, no political influence in state recruitments, and openness to criticism and collective decision making.

The rampant corruption in Africa today is an alien culture, although not an unknown practice. It is very evident that the underdevelopment and rampant corruption in Africa today is a direct consequence of centuries of exploitation by the western Europeans and some African kings. "Before even the western Europeans came into relations with our people, we were a developed people, having our own institutions, having our own ideals of government" (Ekra, 1913.) It is very evident that before the 15th century, when the first European traders traded with Africans, a great civilization was on the move. Dominant pre-colonial African civilizations were Ghana, Mali, Sudan, Nubia, Egypt, Great Zimbabwe, Carthage, and Congo. These kingdoms and empires were never isolated from each other; communications between neighbors, across kingdoms, and beyond the continent were common. Relationships were created through commerce, marriage, migration, diplomacy, and warfare. Eastern kingdoms and empires had come into trade deals with the Chinese, Arab, and Indian traders. The first trade post with the Europeans was established in the 15th century with the Portuguese traders at modern-day Ghana; local surpluses were exchanged for rare foods and goods. East African kingdoms developed the world's prominent marketplaces, and big cities were created at trade junctions like Zanzibar and Timbuktu. Taxes were paid directly to kings and local heads in charge of local commerce. Traders used horses and camels to travel across the continent and beyond to conduct business. Before the 15th century, there were tens of thousands of states and kingdoms in Africa, categorized into centralized and decentralized societies. Rulers and monarchs were at the helm of the centralized societies; they made the laws and collected taxes and comprised just very few people. These states and kingdoms were mostly in agricultural locales and across trade routes.

The power bestowed upon a king or monarch varied from society to society; some kings had all the power of decision-making while some were just more like a symbolic statue. Stronger states and kingdoms gave divine powers to their kings to create strong governmental structures. The Igbo people of modern-day Nigeria and the Kikuyu people of today's Kenya were examples of decentralized societies. People were grouped according to ages and power was given to heads of groups, who then formed the local elders of the societies and closely collaborated with the general public to run the society. Other people grouped up according to their activities, such as the San people of southern African and the pygmy of central Africa, who were migrant hunters. Farming was a vital part of the society as both manpower and metal tools were available to the people; this helped to produce food surpluses, although farming was very unreliable in some areas. Most crop production was maize, yams, or bananas. Other foods, such as cassava, bananas, etc.

were brought by Asians and European traders, and later became a vibrant food source of the societies. Landless families were given or rented farmlands by well-to-do families; as a result, unemployment and homelessness was something very uncommon.

In central and west Africa, societal status was determined by a person's wealth or inheritance. Nobles, royalty, and political leaders were distinguished by great wealth and large residential homes. But widespread flooding often washed away lands and homes, preventing the transfer of wealth from generation to generation. The Dinka people of today's southern Sudan held very low regard for material things. Caution in the running of the governance in both centralized and decentralized societies was never reckoned with because most laws were unwritten, while spirituality and religious dogma attributed disasters to attacks by the gods. This, however, proves the level of emphasis laid on accountability in the running of the state and kingdoms. The rules of law were never reckoned with, like the Asante's kingdom in West Africa.

The Asante kingdoms comprised seven clans and were united by a golden stool of Asante-Hene. According to Dr. Emizet F. Kisangani, the kingdoms (or the "local administration") had in place modernized policies that included supporting advancement by merit and the development of state enterprises through public investment. The Asante were able to build infrastructures supporting agriculture, commerce, industry, and education through self-help and self-reliance. (Chika, 2012.)[7]

In other cultures of Africa, such as the Yoruba people in Nigeria and West Africa, the misuse of power was closely followed by members of the secret house, who were appointed to both choose and swear in kings. If a king was found abusing his power for selfish benefits, the members of the secret house would, in the words of Yunusa Salami, "present him with an empty calabash or parrot's eggs as a sign that he must commit suicide" because, according to tradition, the king could not be deposed.

In other kingdoms, such as in the grass fields of Cameroon, the power of judgment and justice rested in the hands of the chiefs and Fons. It was believed these titled men did not lie; to keep their titles (like the Nobel Prize we have today,) they had to deliver justice; being stripped of their title was a very disgraceful experience. In east Africa, for example, the kingdoms of Great Zimbabwe and Rwanda had very dictatorial caste systems overseen by the king. Justice was given according to which king was in power, but the king never allowed individuals to amass great wealth or land through corruption; anyone suspected of such an act faced the worst punishment from the king.

Such were the practices in place across Africa, but the most important aspect was the values that held these people together, curbing the level of corruption in the administration. Those values were, basically, a set of agreed-upon rules and regulations which comprised the moral values of the societies and guided human interactions. (Chika, 2012.) Earlier proponents of this stance dismissed pre-colonial African achievement and humanity. (Dalgleish, 2005.) These individuals include Hegel, who, in one of his most celebrated works stated "The peculiarly African character is difficult to comprehend, for the very reason that in reference to it, we must give up the principle which naturally accompanies all our ideas –the category of Universality. The Negro exhibits the natural man in his completely wild and untamed state." (Hegel, 1956, 93.)

This paper reviews the literature on corruption, utilizing a holistic approach to analyzing corruption and its economic impact in the world, with emphasis on some countries in Africa, using Nigeria and Cameroon as cases. It analyzes modes and ways of occurrence in various corporate organizations in both developing and developed economies, and includes focus on:

1. *Transparency in corporate organizations.*
2. *Corruption and psychological stress in business circles.*
3. *Is corruption avoidable?*
4. *The corporate ladder –An influence on bribery and corruption.*
5. *Religion and corruption.*
6. *Data corruption.*
7. *Corruption and culture.*
8. *Bribery, corruption, and hiring in the corporate world.*
9. *Human resource management and fraud.*
10. *Good governance for corporate growth.*

New attention to the old problem of corruption has several characteristics.

First, it is international. Previously, corruption was mainly the concern of domestic agencies, like the police or auditors. Now it appears on the agenda of international organizations like the World Bank or the OECD. The internationalization of controlling corruption has been led by a non-government organization, Transparency International (TI), which has campaigned to outlaw the bribery of foreign officials. Transparency International devised a controversial "Corruption Perceptions Index," which ranked countries according to how corrupt they were perceived to be. It followed this up with a Bribe Payers Index, which ranked countries according to their propensity to offer bribes (Transparency International 2000: 13-14.)

Second, it is economical. Previously, corruption was largely the concern of lawyers and criminologists; now, the lead is being taken by economists. They look at the costs of corruption and its effect on economic development (Rose Ackerman, 1999.) They also apply the methods of economic analysis to the problem of corruption, with the assumption that people are rational and calculating, and will respond to incentives and disincentives. This approach is well summarized in Robert Klitgaard's (1988) formula: Monopoly + Discretion − Accountability = Corruption.

Third, the new interest in corruption is less patient with cultural explanations. Previously, corruption in developing countries might be explained by traditions of gift-giving or the obligations of kinship. Now, many people in these countries are less tolerant of such excuses. A draft bill to establish an anti-corruption commission in Papua New Guinea, for example, prescribes bluntly "custom [is] not to be a defense" (Papua New Guinea, 1998, s.40.) This sort of brisk distinction between gifts and bribes has been underscored by the Nigerian

President, Olusegun Obasanjo, who said that the gift is usually a token; it is not demanded. The value is usually in the spirit rather than the material worth. It is usually done in the open, and never secretly. Where it is excessive, it becomes an embarrassment, and it is returned.

If anything, corruption has perverted and destroyed this aspect of our culture (quoted in Pope 1997:5.)

Fourth, corruption is now suspected at the state level, as a state action. Previously, a corruption scandal might lead to a government-sponsored crackdown or inquiry. An "independent" commission might be established, but it would report directly to the Prime Minister or the President. Now, there is more suspicion that those at the top may also be involved. The Independent Commission against Corruption (ICAC) in New South Wales, for example, reports to a bipartisan committee of the legislature, rather than to the government which established it. It investigated the State Premier, leading to his resignation (though the Supreme Court later found the ICAC Act did not apply to the Premier under the circumstances.)

Suspicion of state action has led to a greater emphasis on the role of civil society and the private sector in preventing corruption. Transparency International has supplemented its international action against business corruption by franchising national chapters constituted like any other domestic non-government organization, each campaigning in a different way, monitoring the privatization program in Panama, for example, or establishing advice centers in Bangladesh. Transparency International has also attracted financial support from (among others) large international companies tired of paying bribes. Where the private sector used to be regarded as one cause of corruption, it now casts itself as a victim.

Fifth, it is as much concerned with education and prevention as with investigation and prosecution. Corruption is difficult to investigate. It typically takes place secretly, without witnesses, between willing partners. Prosecution is hard to bring, and there is sometimes suspicion that governments are selectively targeting their political enemies. Like other crimes, more corruption probably takes place than is ever investigated or prosecuted. Additional resources might, therefore, be better spent "upstream," in reforming administrative systems to reduce opportunities for corruption, and in educating citizens against accepting it. Transparency International's mandate specifically precludes it from taking up individual cases.

These five characteristics of the new interest in corruption are linked to broader tendencies. The rapid rise of Transparency International is part of a process of globalization. The involvement of non-governmental organizations (NGOs) and the private sector is characteristic of modern forms of governance, in which order is the result of the interaction between hierarchies, markets, and communities. The economic analysis of corruption is part of a wider intellectual movement to apply the assumptions of rational choice to social and political institutions. There are links between the characteristics, but also tensions between them. Neoliberal economists and NGO activists, for example, may share a suspicion of state action but differ over the value of moralistic appeals. Disciplined secretive organizations like the police force may be uncomfortable with the new emphasis on management reform and civil society.

This paper reflects these new approaches to corruption, but it is also critical of them. It deals with the international dimensions of corruption as human rights issues (Pearson), in the recovery of assets that corrupt leaders have hidden abroad (Chaikin), and in the links between corruption and transnational crime (McFarlane.) It includes an original piece of economic analysis (Menezes.) It is designed to be read by people without formal training in economics and provides a guide to further reading. Other chapters draw on different intellectual and professional traditions, particularly criminology (Grabosky.) Angela Gorta's research for the ICAC draws on broader social-science methodology. Hindess's initial chapter is critical of the narrowness of current economic approaches to understanding corruption, while Warburton's final chapter on corrupt networks draws on politics, sociology, and social psychology.

The title of the paper comes from the ten-point assessment focus treated jointly by my academic/ professional collaborator and myself.

DEFINITION

Corruption is a complex, multi-dimensional concept and difficult to define precisely. Corruption has become a highly topical, international policy issue, and the subject of spectacular research work for scholars of various disciplines like sociology, law, management, economics, public administration, etc.

The word "corruption" comes from the Latin *corruptio*, meaning that which breaks our trustworthiness. The basic meaning of corruption is lack of integrity or honesty, and being unscrupulous, unethical, and untrustworthy.

Corruption points to any ill practice to fulfill a selfish goal. It is a deviation from the value system, derailing individual and institutional transparency, accountability, and natural justice by misusing power and position. Corruption is universal and has existed since time immemorial. It ruins the economic stability of an organization or nation, causing loss of credibility in the administration. Bribes, embezzlement, extortion, kickbacks, theft, fraud, cheating, nepotism, favoritism, adulteration, block money, grease money, misappropriation, and mismanagement are a few forms and ways of representing corruption.

1. Corruption, briefly

There is much talk about corruption, but not everything that is regarded as corruption by the public opinion or mass media is, indeed, corruption. Corruption is not always recognized as a criminal act. Sometimes there is also a superficial perception of the reasons, preconditions, and consequences of corruption and ways to fight it. Therefore, before we analyze corruption, it is worth clarifying the meaning of corruption as a phenomenon.

2. What, then, is corruption?

In early times, the word "corruption" meant decay and moral deterioration. Today, its short definition is **the abuse of public power for personal gain.** The NACP defines corruption as "any behavior of a corporate worker or a civil servant or a person of an equivalent status that is non-compliant with the given powers or established standards of ethics, or the promotion of such behavior, seeking benefit for him or other persons and thus undermining the interests of persons, organizations, and the state." There are many definitions of corruption, and they are constantly subject to change with the changing perception of this phenomenon. Therefore, it is easier to identify corruption by its characteristics, rather than by its definition. Comparison of various concepts of corruption shows that **actions considered as corruption generally incorporate these elements:**

1. A person with the authority (powers) to adopt decisions relevant to society
2. Legal norms regulating decision-making (legislation, principles, criteria, procedures)
3. A person or persons seeking a decision favorable to them
4. The mutually beneficial exchange between a decision-maker and a person or persons seeking this decision
5. Violation of decision-making norms, with consequent damage caused to society [Van Duyne, 2001:74–76]

Corruption is the buying or selling of decisions in violation of justice. Justice can take either a legal form (when a written norm is violated) or a moral one (when there are no established standards of conduct, yet common sense suggests unfairness of an act.)

Following the definitions given above, corrupt decisions are only those that are "sold" by corporate workers, civil servants, and politicians, whereas corruption itself can be public or political. Corruption may also occur in the non-governmental sector and is considered a crime when it violates public interests.

3. Forms of corruption

Decisions sold can affect many matters (provision and facilitation of services, permissions and visas, recruitment and promotion of employees, adoption of laws, abolishment of punishment, concealment of crime, remuneration and other material benefits such as grants, state orders, provision of secret information, exemption from taxes, etc.) In exchange for those decisions, many forms of reward can be offered, ergo, ***there are many forms of corruption, and they are difficult to put into classification.*** What makes the task more difficult is that in different countries, different crimes are considered corruption (bribery is probably an exception.) Crimes of corruption in the legislation of different countries are:

1. Taking, extorting, or giving bribes
2. Mismanagement or embezzlement of state assets
3. Unlawful use of confidential state information
4. Trading in influence and using it for personal benefit
5. Election fraud and interference with elections
6. Dissemination of erroneous information or its provision seeking to mislead investigators
7. Illicit enrichment
8. Obstruction or interference with the market of state orders
9. Punishment of persons who inform about improper conduct of public officials
10. Non-feasance
11. Damage to the public service [Grosse, 2000]

In his attempt to classify the chaotic range of opportunities for corruption, P. Van Duyne suggested a sector-based system [Van Duyne, 2001:76]. This system shows that corruption is possible in all three sectors (public, private and political) and also between them. Based on this model, six groups of crime are possible. The same form of crime (for example, bribes) may occur in every group.

4. Arguments for and against corruption

The first systematic surveys of the consequences of corruption were conducted not long ago. In some, economists and politicians said that corruption was useful, because it:

facilitates decision-making by greasing the wheels of state machinery and hence increasing economic efficiency saves time, and since "time is money," it also saves money transfers the principles of free-market competition into the area of state orders, since the bribes offered while competing for an order show the capacity of the company compensates for the small salaries of civil servants, hence saving budgetary funds. Yet a closer look at the impact of corruption and its level in various countries and their economy shows the negative role that corruption has played in several areas of public life:

- negative impacts on economy
- in corrupt states, the business community must allocate some of its funds to corruption, which cuts down on investment and the gross national product
- corruption binds free competition, with the biggest damage done to small companies
- with decreasing competition, the quality of goods and services becomes worse

- state revenues decrease and the shadow economy grows
- where corruption is tolerated, civil servants receive small salaries, yet with the saved budgetary expenses ordinary citizens must pay them out of their pocket as bribes
- foreign investors have less trust in the state and their contribution to the country's economy decreases
- impact on state governance
- less state investment and smaller efficiency of state-ordered works
- areas of governmental activities and structure of expenditure are subject to change as corrupt public officials "push" the projects which guarantee a bigger gain
- corrupt government is weak and constrained
- selfishness of public officials overshadows strategic thinking in terms of the needs of the state, therefore, economic, and social problems lack proper attention
- the quality of public services deteriorates
- having no trust in corrupt politicians and public officials, citizens lose trust in the state
- there is less involvement in public activities and less interest in the work of democratic bodies
- there is less political competition when autocratic ideologies become more popular
- social tension grows, and the political stability of the state diminishes.

5. What causes corruption?

The fundamental cause of corruption is human egoism. Thus, we cannot consider corruption an exceptional or pathological form of behavior: each and every one of us care about ourselves. The temptation to act in a corrupt manner increases as consumption needs grow and as pursuing personal well-being becomes more important than public well-being: the latter almost slides into oblivion. Corporate experts, politicians, and civil servants abuse their positions to enhance their personal well-being. Observing this, young people perceive civil service as a comfortable and attractive lifestyle. A consumption-oriented society resents corruption scandals, yet its resentment is somewhat double-edged: it is more discontent about someone having bigger gain than about the corruption itself. Yet despite this homogeneity of human nature, societies are not equally corrupt. *The level of corruption may be related to the culture, mentality, and traditions of a certain society.* For example, corruption is more easily perceived as evil by protestant societies because protestant ethics makes a clear distinction between public and individual values. In societies where corruption was almost legal, such as clientelism as a consolidating force in communist systems, it is far more difficult to change living and thinking habits. Corruption takes root more easily in countries where people are less educated and public awareness is low. Corruption may be prompted and maintained by *several social and economic factors:* weak economy, unemployment, poorly administered state budget, or the interference of stronger states and corporations. Civil servants may be demoralized by small salaries, promotion not being linked with the quality of work, an unclear purpose of the organization, and established cliques between superiors and subordinates. Such relations are formed because of low management culture, a lengthy time of service enjoyed by managers, weak control and accountability, and lack of decision-making procedures.

Besides that, the greater the number of goods controlled by the officials and the more secret and monopolized their distribution, the higher the probability of corruption. Another factor determining the level of corruption is *the maturity of the legal system.* Corruption is fostered by unclear, ambiguous, and constantly changing legislation, poorly qualified courts, lack of witness protection programs, and the related mistrust in law enforcement. Therefore, the level of corruption is smaller in the countries with old traditions of statehood, law, and democracy.

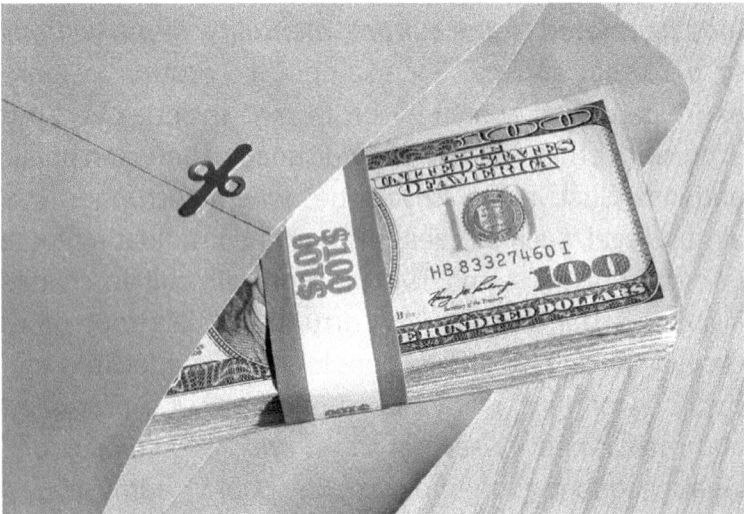

Figure 1. Money in an envelope depicting corruption. Source: Stockmonkeys.com (CC-BY 2.0, 2012)
Source: Stockmonkeys.com (CC-BY 2.0, 2012) Figure 10.1

6. Corruption in International Business

A common practice worldwide is for government favors to be sought in exchange for surreptitious payments in cash. Corruption is not merely a problem in developing countries. In recent years, American, German, and Italian companies have been implicated in corruption scandals, both domestic and international.

7. The Problem of Corruption

When a large corporation enters a foreign market, it must usually secure several licenses, permits, registrations, or other government approvals. Certain types of business may be even impossible or illegal unless the corporation can first obtain a change or adjustment to the nation's laws or regulations. Since the power to authorize the foreign corporation's activities is vested in the hands of local politicians and officials, and since corporations have access to large financial resources, it should not be surprising that some corporate executives resort to financial incentives to influence foreign officials. While certain financial incentives, such as promises to invest in local infrastructure, may be legitimate, any form of direct payment to the foreign official intended to influence that official's public decisions will cross the line into illegal *subornation*, also commonly called *bribery*.

Bribery is one of the archetypal examples of a corporation engaged in unethical behavior. Several problems can be attributed to business bribery.

First, it is obviously illegal —all countries' laws prohibit the bribery of government officials— so the foreign company engaging in bribery exposes its directors, executives, and employees to grave legal risks.

Second, the rules and regulations circumvented by bribery often have a legitimate public purpose, so the corporation may be subverting local social interests and/or harming local competitors.

Third, giving bribes may foment a culture of corruption in a foreign country, which can prove difficult to eradicate.

Fourth, given laws such as the US Foreign Corrupt Practices Act (FCPA) and the Organization of Economic Cooperation and Development (OECD) Convention on Anti-Bribery (discussed in greater detail below), bribery is illegal not only in the target country but also in the corporation's home country.

Fifth, a corporation formally accused or convicted of illicit behavior may suffer a serious public relations backlash.

Despite these considerable disincentives, experts report that worldwide business corruption shows little signs of abating. Transparency International (TI), a leading anti-corruption organization based in Berlin, estimates that one in four people worldwide paid a bribe in 2009. The total continues to increase annually. The World Economic Forum calculated the cost of corruption in 2011 at over five percent of global GDP (US$2.6 trillion), with over $1 trillion paid in bribes each year.

Governments and intergovernmental organizations have redoubled their efforts to combat the perceived increase in international business corruption. Globalization, which accelerated in the final decades of the twentieth century, is often cited by specialists as contributing to the spread of corruption. Corporations and businesses in every nation have become increasingly dependent on global networks of suppliers, partners, customers, and governments. The increased interaction between parties in different countries has multiplied the opportunities for parties to seek advantage from illicit incentives and payoffs. Although outright bribery is unethical and illegal, a great deal of behavior falls into a gray zone that can be difficult to analyze according to a single global standard. When does a business gift become a bribe? What level of business entertainment is "right" or "wrong"? Over the past two decades, governments and regulators have sought to clearly define the behaviors considered unethical and illegal.

Another factor that has heightened the sense of urgency among regulators is the magnitude of recent cases of corruption (several of which are described in greater detail below.) The cost to shareholders, stakeholders, and society has proven enormous. Governments and international organizations have ramped up their enforcement of anti-corruption laws and sought increasingly severe penalties, sometimes imposing fines amounting to hundreds of millions of dollars. Largely because of these efforts, most multinational corporations have developed internal policies to ensure compliance with anti-corruption legislation. However, such compliance also raises complex ethical dilemmas for corporations. It remains difficult to regulate ethical behavior when social and cultural norms vary significantly from country to country. Acts considered unethical in one country may represent a traditional way of doing business in another. One legal scholar explains the difference:

"A common misconception, held in both Western and developing countries, and even among many researchers on corruption, is to confuse what is corrupt with what is legal. Laws are defined by values, as are ethical norms, but the two are not equivalent."

8. The Scope of the Problem

Recent cases of corruption in international business have attracted considerable media attention. Paying a traffic officer to ignore a minor traffic violation is unremarkable; paying a senior government official a secret bribe of millions of dollars to get a large contract signed is a different matter.

While virtually all multinational companies have adopted anti-corruption policies, it is not clear how often these policies are fully implemented and internalized as part of the corporate culture. The emphasis on anti-corruption policies is relatively recent and, even in the most responsible organizations, such policies are still works-in-progress. There is evidence that the implementation is not always as effective as hoped.

For example, a study by Control Risks and the *Economist* magazine's Intelligence Unit showed that while most companies acknowledge the need to combat bribery and corruption, many are complacent and unprepared to deal with scandals inside their own organizations. The review of global attitudes on corruption surveyed over 300 senior lawyers and compliance heads in April of 2013. It painted a disturbing picture. The authors concluded that "too many companies still fall short of best practices in their anti-corruption compliance programs." Despite ranking anti-corruption high on most corporate agendas, the report noted a "danger of complacency" among companies, and "the risk of a company finding itself in the middle of a corruption-based investigation remains real."

Transparency International's Corruption Perceptions Index (CPI) ranks countries and territories according to their perceived levels of public sector corruption. It is an aggregate indicator that combines different sources of information about corruption, making it possible to compare countries. Perceptions are used because corruption is generally a hidden activity difficult to measure. The CPI confirms that corruption remains a problem worldwide and takes place even in the wealthiest countries. Research in 2012 by the Austrian economist Friedrich Schneider placed the annual loss to the German economy alone at €250 billion.

The Dow Jones State of Anti-Corruption Survey in 2011, which surveyed over 300 companies worldwide, found that over 55 percent of companies have found cause to reconsider working with certain global business partners due to concerns about the possible violation of anti-corruption regulations. And the biannual survey indicated that over 40 percent of companies believe they lost business to competitors who won contracts unethically –an increase from only 10 percent in the 2009 study. "Strict liability provisions in legislation like the UK Bribery Act make businesses responsible for the activities of their agents and partners overseas, and this is having a direct impact on the occurrence of new business partnerships between firms," said Rupert de Ruig, managing director of Risk and Compliance, Dow Jones.

Global social costs from corruption include the reluctance of investors to commit to projects in developing economies, inhibited growth of businesses due to siphoning off revenues for bribes, and diversion of funds from food, medical, and educational aid programs. In addition, it seems likely that corruption hampers the development of executive talent in developing nations, given that frustrated local executives may seek to immigrate to countries where corruption is less prevalent. Consider, for example, the long-term impact of the necessity of paying a bribe to get running water in a household in rural India. This corruption can effectively exclude the poor from access to vital public services. Economist Daniel Kaufmann of the Harvard Institute of International Development cites public sector corruption as the most severe obstacle to development in developing and post-communist countries.

9. Notable Examples of Corruption

The number and magnitude of recent corruption cases prosecuted by government authorities are disconcerting. These widely publicized cases may represent only the tip of the iceberg; regulatory bodies focus principally on the bribery of public officials, so other forms of business corruption are under-reported. To date, the ten largest cases successfully tried under the FCPA are listed below (in order of magnitude of fines):

1. Siemens (Germany): $800 million in 2008
2. KBR/Halliburton (USA): $579 million in 2009
3. BAE (UK): $400 million in 2010
4. Total SA (France): $398 million in 2013
5. Snamprogetti Netherlands BV/ENI SpA (Holland/ Italy): $365 million in 2010
6. Technip SA (France): $338 million in 2010
7. JGC Corporation (Japan): $218.8 million in 2011
8. Daimler AG (Germany): $185 million in 2010
9. Alcatel-Lucent (France): $137 million in 2010
10. Magyar Telekom/Deutsche Telekom (Hungary/ Germany): $95 million in 2011

There are other recent examples of large-scale corruption in international business.

10. Walmart in Mexico

According to a report issued by the Mexican Employers Association in 2011, companies operating in Mexico spend over 10 percent of their revenue on corrupt acts. One of the most well-known cases was the Walmart scandal brought to light in September 2005 that resulted in the company's stock value dropping by as much as $4.5 billion. Evidence unearthed by internal and external investigations revealed widespread use of bribes alleged to total over $24 million. The bribes were paid to facilitate the construction of Walmart stores throughout Mexico. The country is a huge market for Walmart; one in every five Walmart stores is in Mexico. As of October 2014, the investigation continued, having implicated Walmart management at the most senior levels of complicity or awareness.

11. GlaxoSmithKline in China

In September 2013, China's Xinhua news agency reported that a police investigation into bribes paid by drug manufacturer GlaxoSmithKline (GSK) indicated that the bribes were organized and paid by GSK China and not by individuals operating on their own prerogative as had been reported by the company initially. Police also alleged that the corporate parent merely went through the motions of an internal audit process, indicating a knowledge and acceptance of the bribery. This very recent case suggests that the Chinese government's widely publicized arrests and convictions for bribery have not yet served as a sufficient deterrent to corrupt practices by foreign corporations.

12. Alcatel in Costa Rica

In January 2010, Alcatel agreed to pay Costa Rica $10 million (USD) in reparations for social damage caused by Alcatel's payment of $2.5 million (USD) in bribes to get a contract to provide mobile phone services in that country. This case is notable for its application of the concept of *social damage* and the resulting order of compensation to the citizens of Costa Rica.

13. Anti-corruption Laws and Regulations

The first major international anti-corruption law was the United States' Foreign Corrupt Practices Act (FCPA), adopted in 1977. The FCPA criminalized bribery of foreign public officials by American business enterprises. Initially, the FCPA was not well received. Few other countries followed, and US companies complained that the FCPA shut them out of the competition for billions of dollars' worth of overseas business contracts. Slowly, however, the push for concerted anti-corruption measures gathered momentum, and intergovernmental institutions such as the OECD, the African Union, and the United Nations eventually adopted anti-corruption conventions. Further support for a global anti-corruption agenda was provided by lending institutions such as the World Bank, by NGOs such as Transparency International, and by the rapidly evolving CSR movement. Notable among these efforts was the Communist Party of China's promulgation of a code of ethics to fight the widespread corruption within the Communist Party of China.

The FCPA applies only to bribes paid (or offered) to foreign government officials to obtain or retain business or to develop an unfair competitive advantage. The concepts of *bribe* and *foreign government official* can be interpreted broadly. While companies and executives charged with FCPA violations have often sought to characterize their payments as business "gifts," this had not shielded them from liability when there was evidence that the payments were intended to obtain illicit objectives. However, where payments have been "facilitation" or "lubrication" payments, meaning they merely created an incentive for an official to promptly execute legal actions such as mandatory customs inspections, the payments have been allowed. In numerous countries, the state owns all or part of commercial enterprises, so that a great number of business executives could be classified as foreign government officials.

In 1997, the OECD established legally binding standards for defining bribery in international business transactions. Similar to the FCPA, the OECD Anti-Bribery Convention focuses on the bribery of public officials. Like the FCPA, the OECD also potentially creates the opportunity for companies to circumvent the regulations by hiring consultants or agents. Notably excluded from the OECD Convention is a prohibition against bribing private parties. Despite such loopholes, the OECD Convention was an important step in the right direction. By 2012, forty-three countries had ratified the agreement and begun its implementation.

(1) TRANSPARENCY IN CORPORATE ORGANISATION

Figure 2. Corporate governance and stake holders

1. Is Transparency the Best Disinfectant?

TRANSPARENCY is a highly regarded value, a precept used for ideological attempts to at least make a show being counter-corruption. Transparency is overvalued, however; its ideological usages cannot be justified, because a social-science analysis shows that transparency *cannot* fulfill the functions its advocates assign to it, although it can play a limited role in their service.

We shall see that in assessing transparency, one must consider a continuum based on the order of disutility and the level of information costs. The higher the score on both variables, the less useful transparency is. These scores need not be high to greatly limit the extent to which the public can rely on transparency for most purposes. Transparency is generally defined as the principle of enabling the public to gain information about the operations and structures of an entity. Transparency is often considered synonymous with openness and disclosure, although one can find subtle differences among these terms. In public discourse, transparency is widely considered as "good" on the face of it, similar to privacy and free speech. Transparency is viewed as a self-evident good in Western society, to the point where we might almost say that "more-transparent-than-thou" has become the secular equivalent of "holier-than-thou" in modern debates over matters of organization and governance. Transparency International, an organization that promotes transparency in many nations, both developing and industrialized, was founded in 1993 and has won much acclaim. Several progressive groups in many democratic countries have been promoting the introduction of "sunshine laws" into legislation.

Reports indicate that transparency has been gaining ground not only in state decision-making bodies but also in states' central banks, the international regimes to which they belong, and even in private companies within their borders. Professor of Government Christopher Hood further documented this trend in a book entitled *Transparency: The Key to Better*

Governance. Transparency has gained additional popularity in recent years since the lack of transparency in financial instruments has been deemed one of the major factors in causing the 2008–2009 near-global economic crises.

Barak Hussein Obama made increasing transparency one of the major themes of his 2008 election campaign. Since his election, there has been a great deal of discussion about the need for more regulation, especially of the financial markets, but so far, little new regulation has been enacted, and various draft bills have encountered a great deal of opposition. In contrast, several transparency measures have been introduced. For instance, the website *Data.gov*, which was launched in May 2009, makes public statistical information collected by over 50 federal agencies. Obama introduced "sunlight before signing", which entails posting new legislation on the web for five days before the president signs the bills into law, to allow for public comments.

Transparency does have an ideological application, one that makes a claim much stronger than the position that transparency is merely one feature of good government. Liberal advocates of transparency maintain that it can obviate the need for most, if not all, government controls. Transparency becomes a tool to fight the regulations imposed by various business groups and politicians from conservative parties. The editorial page of the *Wall Street Journal*, which is openly ideological, runs articles with titles such as "Transparency is More Powerful than Regulations" and lines like "transparency is better than draconian regulation." The importance of the latter article is not where it was published, but who wrote it: Professor Cass Sunstein, a highly regarded scholar appointed by President Obama as the head of the White House Office of Information and Regulatory Affairs (which is in charge of regulations), and Richard Thaler, one of the most respected and influential economists in the United States.

Others advance the argument that better transparency is the surest way to make markets more efficient and less volatile, pointing out that market wisdom results when more people access better information. Some argue that disclosure will allow consumers to become "citizen regulators" and do the job better than the government.

The following analysis deals mainly with transparency in its strong form rather than with its weak, supplementary form. What is at issue is whether transparency can be the mainstay of delivering sought-after goods, rather than whether it can contribute to their promotion. *The critical question is whether transparency constitutes a reliable mechanism of promoting good governance and sound markets under most circumstances, or whether it is a rather weak means that itself relies on other forms of guidance and can supplement regulation but not serve a main form of guidance.* We find that even the soft version, as just an element of regulation, cannot carry much weight.

We need to make two comments to properly focus the following discussion. First, the transparency we deal with here is public and not social. Communitarianism has long ago established that informal social controls can be powerful. People have a profound need for approval from others, especially people to whom they are related by bonds of affection, such as members of their family, social group, or community. For such controls to work, these others must know how an ego is behaving. When people conceal their addictions or abuses from others, social control is often held in abeyance, while disclosure activates it. The mechanisms at work are different from the strong transparency studied in this article; social controls are informal and voluntary. The focus here is on transparency mandated by the government, including annual audited statements by corporations and voluntary associations, campaign contribution disclosure, nutrition and ingredient labels for food, warning labels on hazardous materials, disclosure of terms of contracts and privacy policies, and numerous other transparency mechanisms. This transparency substitutes government regulations for informal social controls.

Secondly, even advocates of strong transparency do not claim it is an absolute value. Clearly, sometimes, transparency must be squared with other values, including security, private property (e.g., trade secrets and copyright protections), and privacy. The best example of the limits of transparency is the rationale for a secret ballot. However, when one is concerned with economic activities, as in this discussion, the majority of laissez-faire conservatives, libertarians, some liberals, and many others hold that (a) the market can regulate itself and (b) if it does need regulation, transparency can provide it.

2. The theory of transparency

Both popular and academic texts lay out how transparency is expected to function. Although they are well known, I review these here to lay out the elements and mechanisms on which transparency is believed to rely. Which, we shall see, essentially are not available.

a. *In the economic realm*

According to the popular version of transparency, consumers control the direction of the economy by using their purchasing power to "vote" on which businesses will succeed and which will fail. For this consumer "sovereignty" to work, consumers must be able to know the attributes of the goods they are about to purchase. This explains the introduction of labels that disclose the attributes of various food items, such as their caloric value, types and levels of vitamins, and so on, and labels on cigarette boxes and posters in liquor stores. The transparency theory presumes that such disclosure will enable consumers to make informed choices, reward the businesses that provide the preferred products, and discourage –even put out of business–those that disregard the informed consumers' preferences.

Transparency has a strong normative underpinning. As Chapman University law professor Susanna Kim Ripken notes, "Respect for individual autonomy, responsibility, and decision-making is deeply entrenched in our culture and law. We believe that people can order their own economic affairs and, given sufficient information, can make their own personal assessments of the risks and benefits of transactions." In addition, she says, "Disclosure promotes fairness and empowers the investor with information to make smart investment choices."

b. *In the public realm*

The same basic argument is a very familiar part of the popular theory of democracy. "Greater openness and wider information-sharing enable the public to make informed political decisions..." writes World Bank economist Tara Vishwanath and the Brookings Institute's Daniel Kaufmann. According to political philosopher Onora O'Neill, transparency "is supposed to discipline institutions and their office-holders by making information about their performance more public. Publicity is taken to deter corruption and poor performance, and to secure a basis for ensuring better and more trustworthy performance." In short, the more strictly we are watched, the better the disclosure of campaign contributions. The Federal Election Commission (FEC), founded in 1975, requires that campaign contributions over $200 to those running for federal office be reported in a timely manner. The McCain-Feingold Act of 2002 requires public disclosure of large donations to political campaigns and was upheld by the Supreme Court in 2003 on the grounds that disclosure of funding is vital for the American citizen to effectively assert his or her right to choose representatives.

Transparency of medical organizations is critical for improving healthcare, according to Sen. Ron Wyden (D-Oregon.). In 1975, *U.S. World and News Report* issued rankings on mortality in various hospitals to allow consumers to select those that performed better and to deny patients to poor performers, assuming such disclosure would either force them to improve their service or close. The same argument was made regarding the disclosure of data about the relative performance of various public schools.

c. *In academic discussions*

A fair number of academic treatments of transparency parallel, and hence at least indirectly support, the popular theory of transparency. These works are much more qualified and nuanced than the ideological texts, although some works, such as those by Milton Friedman, have considerable ideological content. For instance, academic works by economists modify the theory of transparency by introducing transaction costs, such as the cost of collecting and processing information. This element allows one to recognize that consumers and voters may not find it efficient to absorb and process all the disclosed information, and that sub-optimal processing of revealed information may actually make for sub-optimal choices. (This applies to all the cases in which the costs of additional collecting and processing of information, of additional "search," exceed the expected gains.)

Another major addition to the popular theory of transparency is the thesis that the public can utilize intermediaries, experts, technologies, heuristics, and choice architecture to help process the information. As Jason Zweig points out, a 47-page mortgage can lull people into a false sense of security if they mistakenly believe that more details mean more honesty. However, as he sees it, if the industry had to offer a standard mortgage with easy-to-understand terms, consumers might receive less direct information but would gain information they could digest and use. These two brief examples illustrate the point that even when some of the academic work on transparency might be said to support the strong transparency thesis, it does so in a much more qualified way than as seen in transparency's ideological usages.

3. Empirical studies of transparency

Given the high value put on transparency, its ideological currency, and scholarly interest, it is surprising to find there are few empirical studies of the effects of transparency, especially of the strong kind under discussion here. There seem to be no comparative studies of transparency versus other means of regulation, to determine which is more effective. We are hardly the first or only ones who note this. There continues to be a dearth of studies empirically testing the theoretical claims of transparency advocates, even as legislation and institutional support for their case accumulates exponentially. Some of the handful of findings deal with communitarian, not public, transparency, namely of the kind used by communities for their members, which is voluntary in nature rather than imposed by the government. One case in point is the study of "open book" management. With "open book" management, financial information is shared with everyone in a company. The management also lays out the meaning of the financial information and points to ways the employees can contribute to the company's success. A

2005 survey found that 40 percent of the firms among the five hundred fastest-growing private companies employed the practice in some fashion, far more than in the business community as a whole. However, this study dealt with the internal processes of a company, not with the public.

The following are typical findings of the few studies that deal with public transparency.

A study of nutrition labels examined changes in nutrition labeling in grocery stores in New England from 1986 to 1989. It found that such labels affected consumer purchases; however, the effect was small. For instance, the share of household income devoted to milk labeled "healthy" over unlabeled milk rose slightly in the first year. This effect was found only "in those food categories where differences in other quality characteristics (e.g., taste) are relatively small between more and less 'healthy' products." Consumers were only likely to switch to healthier food if the healthy and unhealthy products had similar tastes.

Other studies find that introducing warning labels enhances awareness of risk, but to a rather limited extent. In the first year after introducing alcohol warning labels in 1989, there was a slight increase in the public's perception of the risk associated with consuming alcoholic beverages. About 54 percent of the sample described alcoholic beverages as "very harmful" in 1990, compared to 50 percent of the same a year earlier; the increase was somewhat larger among "heavy" drinkers. Note that this study deals with awareness and perspective, but not with changes in behavior.

A study of disclosure statements in television ads in 2002 found that such disclaimers provide little clari-fication for consumers. A study of the reactions to disclosure statements of 258 undergraduate students over a six-week period, tested disclaimers in multiple ways. The students were explicitly told to pay attention to the disclosure statements, which were then shown multiple times, yet the failure rate for recall remained high. Another scholar concluded regarding political financial disclosures, "There is no empirical evidence that this has resulted in a more aware electorate."

The quality levels of 382 commercial HMOs were observed between 1997 and 2000. The study found that the quality significantly improved among those HMOs that publicly disclosed quality information, "suggesting that public release of quality information can serve as a mechanism to improve quality in healthcare." However, there are very few such studies, and there is no evidence these improvements do not wash out. There are few empirical studies of transparency and several of those that are available deal with communi-tarian rather than government-imposed transparency, or cases wherein the information is easy to collect and process and the change in behavior required to benefit is not taxing. *Most importantly, none of these studies indicate that the effects of transparency are significant enough to obviate the need for regulation, especially where the harm done by an activity or product is consid-erable (relatively high disutility) and the information is relatively complex (that is, the cost of processing the disclosed information is high for the user.)* Given the paucity of empirical studies, we turn next to suggest that strong transparency *cannot* work.

4. A critical examination of transparency

a. *Strong transparency is a form of regulation*

The transparency often discussed as an alternative to regulation is, in effect, a form of regulation because it is required by the government. For instance, corporations are required by law to issue annual statements about their financial activities to the Securities and Exchange Commission. Most food manufacturers are required by the Federal Food, Drug, and Cosmetic Act to place nutrition labels on their products, and so on. Politicians running for federal offices are required by law to post campaign contributions with the FEC. Transparency is "coercive", a label sometimes affixed by opponents to regulation, but which also applies to transparency. Additional regulation is required if the information released to meet the transparency requirements is to be *understandable* to consumers and voters. Unless the government requires disclosure in forms that the public finds digestible, the information is often released in ways that provide little *de facto* transparency. This is an issue with the small, legalistic, and opaque text on the back of airline tickets and when people take out mortgages, credit cards, and auto loans in the United States.

Still more regulation must ensure the *veracity* of the released information. The U.S. Securities and Exchange Commission requires public companies to disclose their financial and operating information as defined by federal statutes, including net sales or operating revenues, income or losses from continuing operations, total assets, long-term obligations, and redeemable preferred stock, every six months in a portfolio snapshot at a particular point. This snapshot can easily be manipulated by readjusting the composition just before and after the snapshot is taken. In the same way, a well-documented practice known as "standardized mortality ratio" (observed after the implementation of requiring hospitals to disclose their mortality rates) most likely reflects the changes in palliative care: fewer patients were admitted to die in the hospital and more patients were discharged to die elsewhere. Political Action Committees (PACs) created by special interest groups regularly adopt names that effectively conceal whom they are promoting. For instance, try to guess to which political party the following PACs are linked: "All America," "America's Foundation," "American Dream," "America Works," and "American Leadership Council." (Answers: D, R, R, D, R.) The same holds true for lobbies that represent various special interests.

Finally, like other regulations, the requirements to be transparent must be *enforced* by the government. Thus, one reason transparency regarding campaign contributions discloses little is that when disclosure laws are violated, the matter goes before the deadlocked, minimally staffed, and poorly funded Federal Election Commission. If the commission does find a grossly misleading disclosure, it is often months too late, well after the election is over.

Regulators failed to impose penalties in almost 500,000 cases of violations of the Clean Water Act by companies that dumped hazardous chemicals in places from which people draw their drinking water.

In short, transparency is merely a form of regulation by other means. These observations are ignored by those who oppose regulation and argue that transparency obviates the need for regulation.

A less dichotomous proposition is more defensible. Regulations come in different shades and forms. For instance, some regulations are more coercive than others: compare those that impose minor fines (like the $20 fine on text messaging while driving in Virginia) to those that require jailing the same offenders. Also, some regulations outright ban certain products or activities, while others merely require that safety measures be added to dangerous products but do not ban them (e.g., seat belts, motorcycle helmets, and, in some jurisdictions, child locks on guns.) In this context, transparency stands out as a relatively light form of regulation, in the sense that meeting its requirements is much less restrictive of producer and consumer choice than other forms of regulations. However, for it to work, consumers and voters must be able to process the released information.

b. *The limits of knowing*
Transparency, unlike other forms of regulation, has a major disadvantage: it assumes those who receive the information released by producers or public officials can properly process it and that their conclusions will lead them to reasonable action. However,

the well-known and often-cited findings of behavioral economics demonstrate that often the public cannot properly process even rather simple information because of "wired in," congenital, systematic cognitive biases. Counterarguments do not seem to hold. The argument that these findings apply only to experimental conditions does not consider the fact that the same limitations have also been demonstrated in field studies. The suggestion that it is rational for people to stop processing information when the cost of additional processing exceeds the benefit assumes that people can correctly assess the cost of information they have not yet collected, but there is next to no evidence that this is the case. None of this is to suggest that providing transparency where it is lacking has none of the desired effects, but merely that often it cannot *by itself* serve the goals set for it, even when consumers and voters must deal with only modestly complex information. And it cannot carry much of the needed public protection under any circumstances. Even the merits of the soft position are greatly limited. In today's "disclosure regime," "Disclosure documents are written by corporate lawyers in formalized language to protect the corporation from liability rather than to provide the investor with meaningful information," notes Susanna Kim Ripken. "The complexity and detail in disclosure documents can make them almost incomprehensible at times... Disclosure cannot fulfill its communicative purpose if investors find it impenetrable and ignore it." Well aware of the fact that transparency mandates *disclosure* or *dissemination*, but does not require effective communication with any audience, these corporate lawyers ignore the fact that "to be effective, information should be fair, reliable, timely, complete, consistent, and presented in clear and simple terms."

Such "fair, reliable, timely, complete, and consistent" disclosure "in clear and simple terms" is rare, and itself requires additional regulation and enforcement. If the released information is to serve the goals set for it, there are often limits on the extent to which it can be simplified, as it contains rather complex assumptions, probabilities, and multiple correlations. Hence, we should not be surprised that it is yet to be demonstrated that even reasonably comprehensive information can still be digested by most people, even those trained in statistics. Behavioral economics and other studies consistently show that often people cannot process even relatively simple information. In response to those who claim that not all investors are "smart," the Efficient Capital Market Hypothesis defends transparency because "the biases, errors in judgments, and decision-making shortcomings of uninformed investors are random and will cancel each other out in the market. Even if people are subject to errors and inconsistencies in decision-making, these fallibilities will be exploited and weeded out of the market by the more sophisticated, rational agents."

However, this theoretical hypothesis is not supported by evidence. Consumers were not protected by "more sophisticated agents" when they were sold sub-prime mortgages they could not pay for, and millions lost their homes; people who rely on brokers or financial advisers for investment advice are doing worse than those who invest in passive investment instruments such as index funds; consumers are not protected by private intermediaries from those who market foods contaminated with E. coli, melamine, or salmonella. Nor, as the record of the last years reminds us, is the whole economic system protected from major crises by such agents. True, other factors are involved, such as irresponsible acts by consumers seeking specu-lative gains in real estate, individuals who consumed more than they earned by using credit cards and so on, tendencies fanned by changes in the culture and by marketing. However, people were not educated about, encouraged to deal with, or protected from these failings by "sophisticated agents." Studies of processing information strongly favor adding stronger forms of regulation than those that merely require transparency even if requirements to communicate are added.

5. Intermediaries: evaluation and trust

a. *Reliance on intermediaries*
Advocates of transparency respond to the findings of behavioral economics by suggesting that people need not process the information because they can rely on experts or leaders –the "smart" members of the masses. For instance, people need not test appliances; they can rely on reports such as those issued by the Consumer Union or on the Good Housekeeping Seal of Approval. Instead of reading long legalistic statements about a corporation's privacy policy on its website, they can rely on the green TRUSTe icon.

However, the issue we face in dealing with the absorbability and veracity of so-called first-order information (and also when dealing with intermediaries) is processed, rather than directly accessed, information. The public does not have the cognitive capacities to determine which intermediary provides better-processed information than another. Reference here is not just to deliberate manipulation, but to differences in the quality of the information processing due to differences in access to primary information, resources available to the analysts, their skills and training, and the assumptions they make. A case in point is the ranking of colleges provided by various publications such as the *US News and World Report*, *USA TODAY*, and the *Princeton Review*, whose lists differ markedly from one another and whose rankings have been subject to considerable controversy. There is no evidence that consumers can evaluate the relative reliability of these rankings any better than they can process the raw information on which these ratings draw.

Hospital rankings have been issued by *US News and World Report* and *Healthinsight.org*, among others, based on data compiled by the Centers for Medicare and Medicaid. Drawing on such processed information, users may well wish to avoid hospitals with high mortality rates. But these are likely to be the best hospitals because they attract patients with severe illnesses. Rankings of high schools issued by *US News and World Report* draw on the number of AP classes taken, which correlates with admission to "elite" colleges. However, these data do not inform the users whether the schools' success is due to the selection of students (i.e., "successful" schools drawing most of their students from affluent neighborhoods which produce more prepared students) or due to the quality of education provided in the school. The users of intermediaries (and the information processed by them) face many of the same problems that individuals encounter when they deal directly with raw information.

Second, the old question of who will guard the guardians applies to intermediaries. As long as they are not regulated, the intermediaries can, and sometimes do, manipulate their rankings. The TRUSTe label is granted to practically anyone who pays for it. Far from indicating that a corporation that displays such an icon provides strong privacy protection, which is how many interpret it, it merely indicates that the corporation is living up to whatever policy it announces, even when the small print states it will sell clients' information to third parties. Perhaps rankings and labels provided by the federal government can be trusted and save the consumer from having to discover the score on their own; however, a report on the USDA's "Organic" label finds that it often applies to products that do not meet consumer expectations of "organic", namely, "foods without pesticides and other chemicals, produced in a way that is gentle to the environment." Instead, many products include ingredients that are neither natural nor environmentally friendly. Consumers and voters cannot evaluate or rely on intermediaries much more than they can rely on the original sources of information, especially if neither is closely regulated.

b. *Information versus choice*
Transparency advocates assume that if given information, individuals will use it to make improved decisions.

Actually, more than a generation ago, we learned that "a curious feature of the growing demand for more information is the paucity of concrete evidence that past disclosures have made significant differences in consumer or market *behavior*." Data from psychological studies show that people "do not make rational choices when it comes to saving and investing activities... information is beneficial only to the extent that it can be understood and utilized by the individual to whom it is directed. Evidence suggests that when people are given too much information in a limited time, the information overload can result in confusion, cognitive strain, and poorer decision-making," concludes Susanna Kim Ripken. A survey found that only 11 percent of Medicare beneficiaries have sufficient knowledge to make an informed choice between new Medicare Choice options and the traditional fee-for-service program. More importantly, in numerous situations even a well-informed person may find choices restricted and must rely on other sources of control for protection. Small investors with pension funds provided by their employers cannot affect the composition of these funds or the selection of funds among which they may choose (if any is provided.)

With health plans, the selection is likely to be even more limited and changes in the plans even less subject to individual preferences. Theoretically, a person could seek another job with the preferred pension or health plan, but the costs of such a shift are often high. Hence, a case can be made that beyond being transparent, pension, and health plans should be mandated to meet at least minimal standards. Even if one disagrees on this point, transparency is limited.

6. The guidance continuum

To reiterate, the question is not, as the *Wall Street Journal* put it, whether "transparency is better than regulation" (which should be "better than other forms of regulation"), but how much of the regulatory mission transparency can carry out. The preceding analysis suggests that it is fairly limited. The main factors that determine the extent to which one can rely on transparency without backing it up it with stronger regulatory means (sometimes referred to as substantive regulation) are: the degree of disutility if the information is not heeded; the education level (whether people are likely to understand the information released); the culture of compliance (whether people trust and heed the information released); and one's values. Clearly, if the harm one seeks to prevent is great when the education level is low, and when there is a strong tendency to ignore or mistrust information released by the government or by corporations, transparency can be relied on even less than if all these factors are reversed. The preceding data suggest that the cutoff point on the continuum these variables form (I call it the guidance continuum) –the point at which transparency cannot be relied upon– is fairly close to the low end of the continuum.

Even if the disutility and distrust are not high, compliance is reasonable, and the level of education is considerable, transparency often will not achieve a reasonable level of public protection. Ultimately, it is a normative issue. If one values autonomy highly and considers it morally acceptable for people to suffer various ill effects if they were informed about the risks involved (or opportunities they miss), one would lean toward relying more on transparency than if one holds that protecting people who cannot protect themselves from serious disutility is morally preferable.

Also, regulations have an "expressive" function; they express the community's shared values and help to set norms. Relying on transparency indicates that the community considers the matter at hand (e.g., public safety, prevention of pandemic, exploitation, manipulation, or fraud) less consequential than if the activities or products are banned, or their provision is required.

7. In conclusion

Transparency is a very popular concept. It implies that people are autonomous, rational choosers who can govern themselves. Theoretically, transparency could be limited to voluntary disclosures. Thus, it could be promoted by consumers refusing to purchase items from sources that do not disclose their content, and investors refraining from investing in corporations that do not provide financial details. Some measure of such voluntary, communitarian disclosure is taking place because it generates goodwill and is considered "good business." However, to ensure the veracity of the information released, to promote releases comprehensible to the public and comparable to information released by other sources, and to secure that such information will be regularly provided, often requires government regulation.

There are few empirical studies of the effects of transparency, and there seem none that compare its effects to other methods of regulation under the same conditions. However, other data, especially evidence assembled by behavioral economists, strongly indicates that people are neither as able to process information nor as likely to act on it as transparency theory presumes. Hence, where adverse outcomes have a relatively high disutility (e.g., they will probably cause death, serious bodily damage, or loss of one's home or life's savings) or the information is complex (e.g., medical information), drawing on other sources of regulation besides transparency seems called for. Transparency cannot replace other kinds of regulation, and even its "soft" version is overrated; it cannot provide much of the public protection, even when combined with other means of regulation.

Finally, from a normative viewpoint, the difference between transparency (which is relatively welcomed by laissez-faire conservatives and libertarians, and by academics whose assumptions parallel these ways of thinking) and other forms of government regulations (which the same sources consider an anathema) is smaller than it at first seems. Under numerous conditions, transparency has to be mandated or it is not provided; the forms of information disclosed must be prescribed, or even the more prepared users cannot decipher the meaning of the released information; and the information's veracity must be assured.

Other kinds of regulation are not necessarily highly coercive. Some merely provide incentives for good conduct. Others impose a minor fine and thus leave it to the regulated agent whether to comply. And for those regulations that outright ban an activity, enforcement varies a great deal. When all is said and done, there is room for increased, validated, and comprehensive transparency (and vetted intermediaries.) However, it is not enough protection when the disutility and the information costs are high, and, often, even when they are not.

(2) CORRUPTION AND PSYCHOLOGICAL STRESS IN BUSINESS CIRCLES

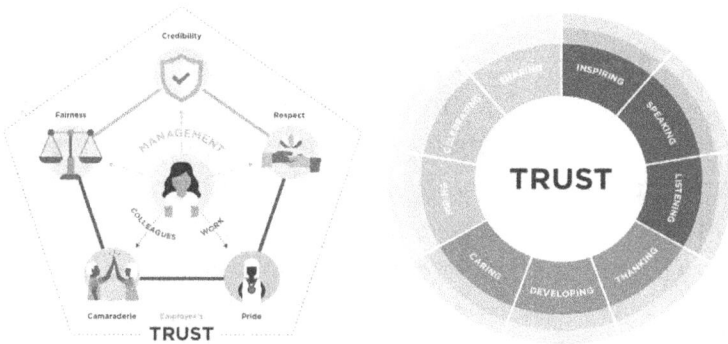

Figure 3. Building trust: psychological stress factor

Occupational stress plays an important role in determining the performance of employees in a company. This occupational stress is heavily influenced by internal factors that originate from within the organization and external factors that originate from outside the organization. Occupational stress can bring about either positive or negative effects on the performance of employees, depending on the level of stress perceived by employees.

Stress is defined in terms of how it impacts physical and psychological health; it includes mental, physical, and emotional strain. Stress occurs when a demand exceeds an individual's coping ability and disrupts his or her psychological equilibrium. Stress occurs in the workplace when an employee perceives a situation to be too strenuous to handle and threatening to his or her well-being.

1. Stress at Work

While it is generally agreed that stress occurs at work, views differ on the roles played by workers' characteristics and working conditions in terms of its primary cause. The differing viewpoints suggest, naturally, different ways to prevent stress at work. Different individual characteristics, like personality and coping skills, can be very important predictors of whether certain job conditions will cause stress. What is stressful for one person may not be a problem for someone else.

Stress-related disorders encompass a broad array of conditions, including psychological disorders (e.g., depression, anxiety, post-traumatic stress disorder) and other types of emotional strain (e.g., dissatisfaction, fatigue, tension), maladaptive behaviors (e.g., aggression, substance abuse), and cognitive impairment (e.g., concentration and memory problems.) Job stress is also associated with various biological reactions such as cardiovascular disease that may ultimately lead to compromised physical health.

2. Categories of Work Stress

Four categories of stressors underlie the different causal circumstances for stress at work:

1. *Task Demands* – This is the sense of not knowing where a job will lead you and whether the activities and tasks will change. This uncertainty causes stress that manifests itself in feelings of lack of control, concern about career progress, and time pressures.
2. *Role Demands* – Role conflict happens when an employee is exposed to inconsistent or difficult expectations. Examples include: inter-role conflict (when there are two or more expectations or separate roles for one person), intra-role conflict (varying expectations of one role), and person-role conflict (ethics are challenged), and role ambiguity (confusion about their experiences in relation to the expectations of others.)
3. *Interpersonal Demands* – Examples include emotional issues (abrasive personalities, offensive co-workers), sexual harassment, and poor leadership (lack of management experience, poor style, inability to handle having power.)
4. *Physical Demands* – Many types of work are physically demanding and may include strenuous activity, extreme working conditions, travel, exposure to hazardous materials, and working in a cramped, loud office.

Causes of Workplace Stress

Work stress is caused by demands and pressure from both within and outside of the workplace.

3. Work-Related Stress

Problems caused by stress have become a major concern to both employers and employees. Symptoms of stress can manifest both physiologically and psychologically. Work-related stress is typically caused by demands and pressure from either within or outside of the workplace; it can be derived from uncertainty over where the job will take the employee, inconsistent or difficult expectations, interpersonal issues, or physical demands.

Although the importance of individual differences cannot be ignored, scientific evidence suggests that certain working conditions are stressful to most people. Such evidence argues that working conditions are a key source of job stress and job redesign should be a primary prevention strategy.

4. Studies of Work-Related Stress

Large-scale surveys of working conditions, including conditions recognized as risk factors for job stress, were conducted in member states of the European Union in 1990, 1995, and 2000. Results showed a time-related trend that suggested an increase in work intensity. In 1990, the percentage of workers reporting they worked at high speeds for at least one-quarter of their working time was 48%; this increased to 54% in 1995 and 56% in 2000. Similarly, 50% of workers reported that they worked against tight deadlines at least one-fourth of their working time in 1990; this increased to 56% in 1995 and 60% in 2000. However, no change was noted in the period from 1995 to 2000 in the percentage of workers reporting enough time to complete tasks (data was not collected in 1990 for this category.)

A substantial percentage of Americans work long hours. By one estimate, over 26% of men and over 11% of women worked 50 hours or more per week (outside of the home) in 2000. These figures represent a considerable increase over the previous three decades, especially for women. According to the Department of Labor, there has been an upward trend in hours worked among employed women, an increase in work-weeks of greater than forty hours by men, and a considerable increase in combined working hours among working couples, particularly couples with young children.

5. Power and Stress

A person's status in the workplace can also affect levels of stress. Stress in the workplace has the potential to affect employees of all categories, and managers and other kinds of workers are vulnerable to work overload. However, less powerful employees (those with less control over their jobs) are more likely to experience stress than employees with more power. This indicates that authority is an important factor complicating the work stress environment.

6. Economics and Stress

Economic factors that employees are facing in the 21st century have been linked to increased stress levels. Researchers and social commentators have pointed out that advances in technology and communications have made companies more efficient and more productive than ever before. This increase in productivity has resulted in higher expectations and greater competition, which place more stress on employees.

- These economic factors can contribute to workplace stress include:
- Pressure from investors who can quickly withdraw their money from company stocks
- Lack of trade and professional unions in the workplace
- Inter-company rivalries caused by global competition
- The willingness of companies to swiftly lay off workers to cope with changing business environments

7. Social Interactions and Stress

Bullying in the workplace can also contribute to stress. Workplace bullying can involve threats to an employee's professional or personal image or status, deliberate isolation, or giving an employee excess work.

Another type of workplace bullying is known as "destabilization." Destabilization can occur when an employee is not given credit for their work or is assigned meaningless tasks. Destabilization can create a hostile work environment for employees, negatively affecting their work ethic and, therefore, their contributions to the organization.

8. Stress Outside of the Workplace

Non-work demands can create stress both inside and outside of work. Stress is inherently cumulative, and it's difficult to separate personal and professional stress inducers. Examples of non-work stress that can be carried into the workplace include:

- *Home demands:* Relationships, children, and family responsibilities can add stress hard to leave behind when entering the workplace. The *Academy of Management Journal* states this constitutes "an individual's lack of personal resources needed to fulfill commitments, obligations, or requirements."
- *Personal demands:* Personal demands are brought on by the person when he or she takes on too many responsibilities, either inside or outside of work.

9. Consequences of Workplace Stress

Stress can affect an individual mentally and physically and so can decrease employee efficiency and job satisfaction.

10. Stress

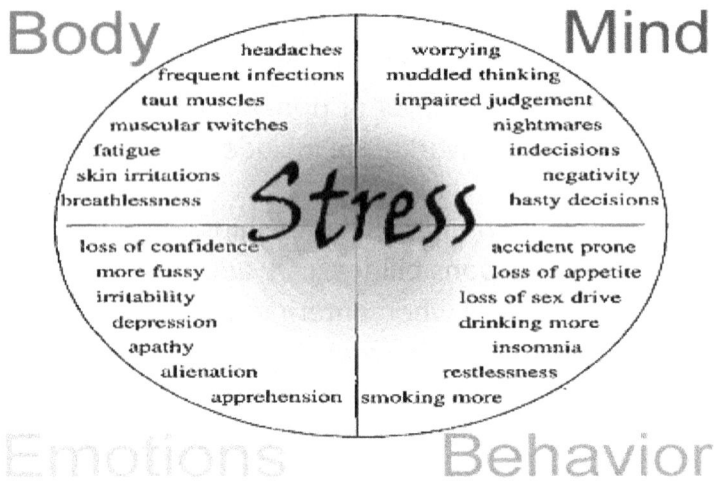

Figure 4. Stress components in workplace

11. Symptoms of stress

Stress can manifest as various symptoms affecting one's body, mind, behavior, and/or emotions. Negative or overwhelming work experiences can cause a person substantial distress. Burnout, depression, and psychosomatic disorders are common outcomes of work-related stress. Individual distress manifests in three basic forms: psychological disorders, medical illnesses, and behavioral problems.

12. Psychological Disorders

Psychosomatic disorders are a type of psychological disorder. They are physical problems with a psychological cause. For example, a person extremely anxious about public speaking might feel nauseated or may find them unable to speak at all when faced with the prospect of presenting in front of a group. Since stress is often difficult to notice, managers would benefit from carefully monitoring employee behavior for indications of discomfort or stress.

13. Medical Illnesses

Physiological reactions to stress can have a long-term impact on physical health. Stress is one of the leading precursors to long-term health issues. Backaches, stroke, heart disease, and peptic ulcers are just a few physical ailments that can arise when a person is under too much stress.

14. Behavioral Problems

A person can also exhibit behavioral problems when under stress, such as aggression, substance abuse, absenteeism, poor decision making, lack of creativity, or even sabotage. A stressed worker may neglect their duties, impeding workflows and processes so the broader organization slows down and loses time and money. Managers should keep an eye out for such behaviors as possible indicators of workplace stress.

15. Organizational Effects of Stress

Stress in the workplace can be, so to speak, "contagious"; low job satisfaction is often something employees will discuss with one another. If stress is not noted and addressed by management early on, team dynamics can erode, hurting the social and cultural synergies present in the organization. Ultimately, the aggressive mentality will be difficult to remedy.

Managers are in a unique position to deal with workplace stress. As they set the pace, assign tasks, and foster the social customs that govern the work group, management must know the repercussions of mismanaging and inducing stress. Managers should consistently discuss job satisfaction and professional and personal health with each of their subordinates one on one.

16. Reducing Workplace Stress

A combination of organizational change and stress management is a productive approach to preventing stress at work. Stress management refers to a wide spectrum of techniques and therapies that aim to control a person's levels of stress, especially chronic stress, to improve everyday functioning.

17. Preventing Job Stress

If employees are experiencing unhealthy levels of stress, a manager can bring in an objective outsider, such as a consultant, to suggest a fresh approach. But there are many ways managers can prevent job stress. A combination of organizational change and stress management is often the most effective approach. Among the many techniques managers can use to effectively prevent employee stress, the main underlying themes are awareness of possibly stressful elements of the workplace and intervention when necessary to mitigate any stress that does arise.

Specifically, organizations can prevent employee stress in these ways:

18. Intentional Job Design

- Design jobs that provide meaning and stimulation for workers and opportunities for them to use their skills
- Establish work schedules compatible with demands and responsibilities outside the job
- Consider flexible schedules; many organizations allow telecommuting to reduce the pressure of being a certain place at a certain time (which enables people to better balance their personal lives)
- Monitor each employee's workload to ensure it is in line with their capabilities and resources

19. Clear and Open Communication

- Teach employees about stress awareness and promote an open dialogue
- Avoid ambiguity at all costs; clearly define workers' roles and responsibilities
- Reduce uncertainty about career development and future employment prospects

20. Positive Workplace Culture

- Provide opportunities for social interaction among workers
- Watch for signs of dissatisfaction or bullying, and work to combat workplace discrimination (based on race, gender, national origin, religion, or language)

21. Employee Accountability

- Give workers opportunities to participate in decisions and actions that affect their jobs
- Introduce a participative leadership style and involve as many subordinates as possible in resolving stress-producing problems

(3) IS CORRUPTION AVOIDABLE?

You can stop
COR RUPTION

1. Overcoming corruption

The first generation of anti-corruption measures taken in the mid-1990s by finance-development institutions involved ambitious efforts to overhaul civil service systems along Weberian lines, incentivizing officials by increasing wage dispersion and setting formal recruitment and promotion criteria. These measures had little effect; the problem lay in corrupt organizations being expected to police themselves and to implement bureaucratic systems developed over long periods in rich countries with very different histories. More recent efforts have focused on fighting corruption through transparency and accountability measures – increasing the monitoring of agent behavior and creating positive and negative incentives for better compliance with the institution's goals. This has taken a variety of forms: cameras placed in classrooms to ensure that teachers show up for work; participatory budgeting where citizens are given a direct voice in budgeting decisions; and websites where citizens can report corporate officials taking bribes. Since governments cannot be trusted to police themselves, civil society has often been enlisted in a watchdog role and mobilized to demand accountability. Mechanisms like anti-corruption commissions and special prosecutors have, if given enough autonomy, also shown success in countries such as Indonesia and Romania.

These later efforts, however, have also had uneven success (see, for example, Kolstad and Wiig, 2009; Mauro, 2002.) Transparency initiatives by themselves do not guarantee changes in corporate or government behavior. For example, in countries where clienteles are organized along ethnic lines, co-ethnics are frequently tolerant of leaders who steal. Elsewhere, citizens may be outraged by news of corruption, but then have no clear way of holding individual politicians or bureaucrats accountable. In other cases, successes in punishing individual politicians cannot shift the normative framework in which virtually everyone in the political class expects to profit from office. Finally, anti-corruption campaigns may disrupt informal understandings and personal relationships that underpin investment and trade: without formal property rights and contract enforcement under a system of independent courts, the paradoxical short-term effect of prosecuting corrupt officials may be to deter new investment and lower growth.

A single truth underlies the indifferent success of existing transparency and accountability measures to control corruption: the sources of corruption are deeply political. Without a political strategy for overcoming this problem, any given solution will fail. Corruption in its various forms –patronage, clienteles, rent-seeking and outright theft– all benefit existing stakeholders in the political system who are generally very powerful players. Lecturing them about good government or setting up formal systems designed to work in modern political systems will not affect their incentives and will have little transformative effect. That is why transparency initiatives on their own often fail. Citizens may be outraged by news about corruption, but nothing will happen without collective-action mechanisms to bring about change. The mere existence of a democratic political system is no guarantee that citizens' anger will be translated into action; they need leadership and a strategy for displacing entrenched stakeholders from power. Outside pressure in the form of loan conditionality, technical assistance, or moral pressure is rarely sufficient to do the job. Anti-corruption commissions and special prosecutors who have had success in jailing corrupt officials have done so only because they receive strong grassroots political backing from citizens.

2. The American experience

The political nature of corruption and the necessarily political nature of the reform process can be illustrated by the experience of the United States in the 19th century (Fukuyama, 2014, chapters 9–11.) American politics in that period was not too different from politics in contemporary developing democratic countries such as India, Brazil, or Indonesia. Beginning in the 1820s,

American states extended the franchise to include all white males, expanding the voter base and presenting politicians with the challenge of mobilizing relatively poor and poorly educated voters. The solution, which appeared after the 1828 presidential election that brought Andrew Jackson to power, was the creation of a vast clientelist system. Elected politicians appointed their supporters to positions in the bureaucracy or rewarded them with individual payoffs like Christmas turkeys or bottles of bourbon. This system, known as the spoils or patronage system, characterized American government and their organizations for the next century, from the highest federal offices down to local postmasters in every American town or city. As with other clientelist systems, patronage led to astonishing levels of corruption, particularly in cities such as New York, Boston, and Chicago where machine politicians ruled for generations.

This system changed only in the 1880s, due to economic development. New technologies like the railroads were transforming the country from a primarily agrarian society into an urban industrial one. There were increasing demands from business leaders and from a newly- emerging civil society for a different, more modern form of government that would priori- tize merit and knowledge over political connections. Following the assassination of the newly elected President James A. Garfield in 1881 by a would-be office seeker, Congress was embarrassed into passing the Pendleton Act. It established a U.S. Civil Service Commission to promulgate the principle that public officials should be chosen based on merit. Expanding the number of classified (i.e. merit-based) officials met strong resistance and did not become widespread until after the First World War. Individual municipal political machines such as Tammany Hall in New York were not dismantled completely until the middle of the 20th century.

The American experience highlights several features of both corruption and the reform of corrupt systems. First, the incentives that helped to create the clientelist system were deeply political. Politicians got into office via their ability to distribute patronage; they had no incentive to vote for something like the Pendleton Act that would take away those privileges. The only reason it passed was a tragic exogenous event –the Garfield assassination– which mobilized public opinion for a more modern governmental system.

Second, reform of the system was similarly political. The Progressive Era saw the emergence of a vast reform coalition made up of business leaders, urban reformers, farmers, and ordinary citizens fed up with the existing patronage system. It required strong leadership from politicians like Theodore Roosevelt, who was himself head of the U.S. Civil Service Commission. It also required a clear reform agenda pointing towards modern government, formulated by intellectuals such as Frank Goodnow, Dorman Eaton, and Woodrow Wilson.

Finally, reform was helped along by economic development. Industrialization in the US produced new social groups such as business leaders who needed efficient government services, a broad and better-educated middle class who could mobilize for reform, and a grassroots organization of civil society groups.

3. Conclusions

The American experience suggests how progress in the fight against corruption may be waged in contemporary societies suffering from it. Reform is always a political matter that will require formation of a broad coalition of groups opposed to an existing system of corrupt politicians. Grassroots activism for reform may emerge spontaneously, but such sentiments will not be translated into real change until it receives good leadership and organization. Reform also has a socio-economic basis: economic growth often produces new classes and groups that want different, more modern politics.

The American experience also points to another feature of anti-corruption efforts. Control of corruption was very much bound up with efforts to increase state capacity. The period that saw the emergence of an industrial economy was also characterized by huge increases in levels of education, particularly higher education, which produced a new class of professionals who worked for both private businesses and the government. One of the first government agencies to be modernized in the late 19th century was the U.S. Department of Agriculture, which benefited from a generation of professional agronomists trained in the numerous land-grant universities that sprang up around the United States. The latter, in turn, were the product of the far-sighted Morrill Act of 1862 that sought to increase agricultural productivity through higher education.

It would not have been possible to reform the old patronage-based bureaucracy without access to the human capital represented by this entire generation of university-educated officials. Every important reform effort undertaken to create modern state bureaucracies –in Germany, Britain, France, Japan and elsewhere– came with parallel efforts to modernize the higher education system in ways that would benefit public administration. Today development finance institutions focus on helping to educate poor countries and have largely given up on supporting elite education. The reasons for this are understandable, but do not correspond to the historical experience of state modernization in countries that became rich in earlier eras.

These general observations about historical efforts to build modern uncorrupt administrations suggest that the process will be an extended one, characterized by prolonged political struggle. Fortunately, having a modern bureaucracy is not a sine qua non of economic development. No existing rich country had a squeaky-clean government in its early stages of economic growth; neither Britain, nor the United States in the 19th century, nor China today. Corruption and weak governance are obstacles to economic growth, but economic growth can happen also in poorly governed societies and will produce, over time, social conditions and resources that will make government reform more feasible. This is perhaps a pessimistic conclusion, because rentier states and kleptocratic governments are the source of international conflict and instability in today's world. But it is also a realistic assessment derived from the historical record.

(4) THE CORPORATE LADDER –AN INFLUENCE ON BRIBERY AND CORRUPTION

Corruption can affect all aspects of HR management processes, with favoritism and nepotism and abuse of authority in areas of recruitment, training, promotion, and transfer identified as major risk areas. This is rendered possible by unchecked discretionary power as well as lack of integrity and/or accountability, checks and balances, and transparency in the overall administration of HR services. Buying and selling positions, nepotism, patronage and corruption in recruitment and promotion are major concerns in many developing countries' public sectors. Such practices result in employing unqualified civil servants, fueling the development of corrupt patronage networks within the public service, and undermining the goal of building strong and efficient bureaucracies.

1. Selling or buying positions

Buying and selling positions is common in many countries, especially positions considered as lucrative and providing opportunities for illicit enrichment. In Benin and Senegal for example, the most "attractive" postings are at border crossings with a high density of transactions and interaction with the public, followed by those at the ports, the airports, and postings at busy road intersections (Feldstad, 2009.) In China, corruption in selling civil posts is also widespread, especially in local governments (Poocharoen and Brillantes 2013.)

Political patronage and nepotism based on kinship ties or political allegiance, depending on the local context, are also common practices in many developing countries. In the absence of fair and transparent recruitment processes, officials can use their discretionary powers to employ and promote friends, relatives. or political supporters to public jobs they would not get otherwise. While some countries have central examinations in place to address this challenge, this does not necessarily eliminate risks of favoritism in the hiring process, as favoritism may occur after the central examination takes place. For example, insiders may leak the exam questions to their favorite candidates. At the interview stage, those with the better connections may be better rated, with sons and daughters of the elite families receiving preferential treatment (Poocharoen and Brillantes, 2013.) In some countries, such as Philippines and Malaysia, recommendations from government officials are used as selection criteria. Such practices can be misused, leading to patron-client relationships wherein the person hired feels indebted to the person who made the recommendation (Poocharoen and Brillantes, 2013.) There is also a growing trend in many public administrations to make contract-based rather than tenure appointments, with more discretion on how to select, who to select, and the terms of the appointments (Poocharoen and Brillantes 2013.)

Political affiliation can play an important role in the appointment of civil servants, leading to the politicization of the public sector, as political parties have incentives to gain control over bureaucrats. Some countries implicitly or explicitly make party membership a prerequisite for joining the civil service, and this is often accepted as a hidden norm. In China, for example, communist party members make up 5% of the population but hold 80% of the civil service posts. In Singapore, the People's Association Party has a strong hold on appointments of all leading positions in government. In the Philippines, in a survey of high-ranking civil servants, the majority (77%) of respondents indicated there is interference or pressure by politicians or other influential persons in the hiring process (Poocharoen and Brillantes, 2013.)

2. Performance management, transfers, and promotions

Weak incentive structures in the civil service under-mine good performance and result in a weak work ethic and poor service delivery. Public administrations often restrict certain promotions to existing staff to minimize costs and provide career development opportunities. Internal promotion and transfers may provide opportu-nities for favoritism, as managers have typically greater discretion in performance management and promo-tion. In countries where selection is based on merit, promotion and rotation opportunities may be tied to political loyalties. In Thailand, for example, elected politicians can gain control over bureaucrats through interventions in promotion processes, as ministers have tremendous power to nominate and approve promotion to key positions such as permanent secre-taries, directors, and deputy directors in key agencies (Poocharoen and Brillantes, 2013.) Staff transfers can also be misused by corrupt managers as a reward or punishment for honesty. In some countries, rotation systems of staff have been introduced to limit opportu-nities for staff in "lucrative" positions, such as customs, to develop corrupt networks in their interactions with service users. The rotation of officials may also give corrupt superiors undue power. For instance, they might "sell" assignments to attractive positions or reassign officials to remote stations as a punishment for honesty. Rotation may also create incentives for staff to enrich themselves as much as they can while they are stationed in the most "lucrative" posts (Feldstad, 2009.)

3. Revolving doors

Increased mobility between private and public sectors also raises the risks of revolving doors or policy capture, when ex-government officials go to work for the sectors they used to regulate. While some argue that the practice of moving back and forth between the public and private sectors equips regulators and policy makers with specialized knowledge and practical insights into very complex technical issues and processes, there are indications they are often hired not for their competence but for their connections and special access acquired while working in government (Zinnbauer, 2014.) This practice seems to be on the rise in many countries. For example, examining the career trajectories of members of Congress in the US, LaPira and Thomas (2012) found that while less than 10% of Congress members in the 1970s left to become lobbyists, more than half of all Congress members who left in 2012 have registered as lobbyists. While such practices are not unlawful, this revolving door may lead to conflicts of interest, regulatory capture, and corruption both during and after a regulator's term in public office, as corroborated by several cross-country analyses and case studies (Brezis and Cariolle, 2014.)

Compensation and benefits

4. Low salaries and corruption

In many developing countries, public service wages have declined rapidly over the past two decades. Due to a lack of resources and fiscal adjustment policies in stabilization programs, public-service salaries and conditions have fallen far behind the private sector, with a trend of growing differentials between public and private sector wages (Chêne, 2009.) There is a broad consensus that low salaries and weak monitoring systems are breeding grounds for corruption, as underpaid staff develop individual coping strategies to top off their income with activities such as teaching, consulting for development agencies, operating private businesses, moonlighting in the private sector, or benefiting from generous systems of donor-funded per diems and allowances. Corruption can also be a coping strategy to compensate for economic hardship, with underpaid officials demanding bribes or informal payments for services supposed to be free or misusing public resources for private gain. In such a context, there is greater public tolerance for "need-based" forms of corruption, when civil servants' wages are below the living standards or perceived as unfair compared to private sector salaries. Declining wages and purchasing power also make it difficult for the public sector to attract and retain honest, qualified and motivated staff, resulting in draining highly qualified staff away from government and into the private sector, which offers better pay incentives and career opportunities.

5. High salaries and corruption

In theory, higher salaries may reduce incentives for "need-based" forms of corruption. They also may make corruption more costly, as corrupt behavior increases the risk of losing a highly rewarding job. However, evidence is inconclusive as to whether increasing salaries without establishing effective control and monitoring systems and increasing the risk of getting caught is an effective anti-corruption approach (Chêne, 2009.)

In addition, when the HR management lacks transparency and a standardized compensation framework, increasing salaries can open the door to favoritism, abuse, and "institutionalized" predation. In Zimbabwe, for example, in 2014, the country was hit by a salary scam −called "Salary-gate"− involving senior executives in state-owned enterprises and other public entities, who had awarded themselves exorbitant salaries despite poor economic performance. For instance, senior officials of the Zimbabwe Broadcasting Corporation awarded themselves hefty salaries each month, enjoying unlimited access to fuel and air travel, while their employees went unpaid for more than half a year. HR managers were also implicated in the scam (Ncube, 2014.)

6. Per diems and allowances

Per diems consisting of daily payments made by organizations to cover employees' expenses incurred in work related activities have been used in many countries as a coping strategy to compensate for low public-sector wages. Such practices proved extremely costly for governments in developing countries. In Tanzania, for example, the amount allocated for allowances for the fiscal year 2009/2010 represented 59% of the total wage bill (Policy Forum, 2009.) There are many opportunities for abusing the per diem regime. Allowances can be paid at a rate higher than the specified rates or paid to staff not entitled to them. High-level officials can also misuse the lucrative system of per diems and allowances for their own benefit. Donor-funded projects can be manipulated by public officials to sustain their patronage network and reinforce client-patron relationships. Work practices can be manipulated, by slowing down work, scheduling unnecessary training or exaggerating the time needed for tasks. Per diems are also vulnerable to theft or workshop-related fraud. Interviews conducted with government and non-governmental officials in Malawi and Uganda revealed that allowances were perceived as providing unfair advantages to already better-off and well-connected staff (Vian & al, 2011.)

Meritocracy

7. Merit–based recruitment and promotion:

There is a broad consensus that promotion and recruitment to the civil service should be based on merit, not political or family connections, with the view to making public administration more professional and

efficient. However, there is no consensus on the definition of "merit" and the best tools to assess the concept
of "merit." It is important to precisely define "merit"
in terms of knowledge and skills. If merit is vaguely
defined in broad terms, such as "able to do the job",
many candidates may be adequate and the ambiguity
may be misused to favor relatives or political supporters
to the detriment of other outstanding candidates
(McCourt, 1999; Poocharoen and Brillantes, 2013.)
In many countries, building merit-based civil service
systems often includes basic university degree requirements and/or a central open-examination competition.
However, having entry exams does not necessarily
translate into employees feeling that meritocracy is
practiced. For example, in South Korea and Taiwan,
while there are stringent exams for entering civil
service, only 35% of a survey's respondents agreed
that merit principles are used in actual hiring processes
(Poocharoen and Brillantes, 2013.)

Entry-level exams are not the only tool to ensure
merit-based recruitment and must come with other
selection tools. In the Philippines, for example, recruitment criteria are shifting from requiring minimum levels
of education, training, and work experience to include
value dimensions, such as integrity, honesty, and work
ethics. As qualifications are only to a limited extent
correlated to job performance, some countries such as
the U.S. put more emphasis on work experience than
on written exams, reflecting a selection process based
on interviews allowing selection to be based on competencies (Poocharoen and Brillantes, 2013.) Irrespective
of the selection process, appointment policy should

include several steps: 1) a job analysis/description, 2) an advertisement to eligible groups, 3) a standard application process, 4) a scoring scheme, 5) a short-listing procedure, 6) a final selection procedure, 7) an appointment procedure; and, 8) notification of results to successful and unsuccessful candidates. Institutional arrangements should be considered to separate the administrative sphere from the political sphere, so it protects appointments from any form of undue political interference (McCourt, 1999.)

8. Merit-based appraisal systems and performance management

Similarly, performance management should be transparent and based on clear and objective criteria, to limit the managers' discretion. While performance may be considered in setting pay, or bonus levels, those settings must be based on actual performance, objectively assessed and properly documented (Whitton, 2001.) At service-delivery level, performance management may involve regular monitoring of staff attendance, especially in countries with high levels of absenteeism. In some countries, such as Kenya and Uganda for example, direct observation of teacher attendance has been used, relying on unannounced visits to address absenteeism (World Bank, 2010.) The Philippines has set up a performance management system that links individual performance with organizational performance, to create a rating system that can assess individual performance for better decisions on tenure, promotion, and rewards (Poocharoen and

Brillantes, 2013.) An institution that wishes to set clear ethical standards can also use appraisal systems to reinforce its strong stance against corruption by integrating ethical behavior indicators into the performance review process. Such indicators are typically sector specific and need to follow the organization's set of values and policies, as reflected in a guide for building workplace integrity developed by Australia's Office for Police Integrity (Office of Police Integrity, 2009.)

(5) DATA CORRUPTION

One of the biggest challenges in designing storage systems is providing the reliability and availability that users expect. Once their data is stored, users expect it to be reliable forever and perpetually available. Unfortunately, in practice, there are several problems that, *if not dealt with, can cause data loss in storage systems.

One primary cause of data loss is disk drive unreliability. It is well-known that hard drives are mechanical, moving devices that can suffer from mechanical problems leading to drive failure and data loss. For example, media imperfections, and loose particles causing scratches, contribute to media errors (called latent sector errors), within disk drives. Latent sector errors are detected by a drive's internal error-correcting codes (ECC) and are reported to the storage system.

Less well-known, however, is that current hard drives and controllers consist of hundreds of thousands of lines of low-level firmware code. This firmware code, along with higher-level system software, has the potential for harboring bugs that can cause a more insidious type of disk error, "silent data corruption", where the data is silently corrupted with no indication from the drive that an error has occurred.

Silent data corruption can lead to data loss more often than latent sector errors, since, unlike latent sector errors, they cannot be detected or repaired by the disk drive itself. Detecting and recovering from data corruption requires protection techniques beyond those provided by the disk drive. Basic protection schemes such as RAID may detect these problems.

The most common technique used in storage systems to detect data corruption is for the storage system to add its own higher-level checksum for each disk block, which is validated on each disk block read. There is a long history of enterprise-class storage systems using checksums in a variety of manners to detect data corruption. However, as we discuss later, checksums do not protect against all forms of corruption. Therefore, besides checksums, some storage systems also use system-level disk-block-identity information to detect previously undetectable corruptions.

To further improve on techniques to handle corruption, we need to develop a thorough understanding of data corruption characteristics. While recent studies provide information on whole disk failures and latent sector errors that can aid system designers in handling these error conditions, little is known about data corruption, its prevalence, and its characteristics. This paper presents a large-scale study of silent data corruption based on field data from over a long period of time. We use the same data set as the one used in recent studies of latent sector errors and disk failures. We identify the fraction of disks that develop corruption, examine factors that might affect the prevalence of corruption, such as disk class and age, and study characteristics of corruption, such as spatial and temporal locality. To the best of our knowledge, this is one of the first studies of silent data corruption in production and development systems.

(i) We classify data corruption into three categories based on how it is discovered: checksum mismatches, identity discrepancies, and parity inconsistencies (described below.) We focus on checksum mismatches since they are found to occur the most. Our important observations include:

(ii) *During this period, we observe more instances of checksum mismatches, 8% of which were discovered during RAID reconstruction, creating the possibility of real data loss. Even though the rate of corruption is low, the discovery of checksum mismatches during reconstruction illustrates that data corruption is a real problem that needs to be considered by storage system designers.*

(iii)*We find that near-line (SATA) disks and their adapters develop checksum mismatches more often than enterprise-class (FC) disks, while enterprise-class disks develop more checksum mismatches than near-line disks.*

(iv) *Checksum mismatches are not independent occurrences, being found both within a disk and within different disks in the same storage system.*

(v) *Checksum mismatches have tremendous spatial locality; on disks with multiple mismatches, it is often consecutive blocks that are affected.*

(vi)*Identity discrepancies and parity inconsistencies do occur but affect 3-to-10 times fewer disks than checksum mismatches do.*

1.Storage System Architecture

The data we analyze is from tens of thousands of production and development Network Appliance TM storage systems (henceforth called *the system*) installed at hundreds of customer sites. This section describes the architecture of the system, its corruption detection mechanisms, and the classes of corruption in our study.

Storage Stack

Physically, the system comprises a storage-controller that contains the CPU, memory, network interfaces, and storage adapters. The storage-controller is connected to a set of disk shelves via Fiber Channel loops. The disk shelves house individual disk drives. The disks may either be enterprise class FC disk drives or near-line serial ATA (SATA) disks. Near-line drives use hardware adapters to convert the SATA interface to the Fiber Channel protocol. Thus, the storage-controller views all drives as being Fiber Channel (however, for the study, we can still identify whether a drive is SATA or FC by using its model type.)

The software stack on the storage-controller comprises the WAFL® file system, RAID, and storage layers. The file system processes client requests by issuing read and write operations to the RAID layer, which transforms the file system requests into logical disk block requests and issues them to the storage layer. The RAID layer also generates parity for writes and reconstructs data after failures. The storage layer is a set of customized device drivers that communicate with physical disks using the SCSI command set.

2. Corruption Detection Mechanisms

(a) Format for enterprise class disks

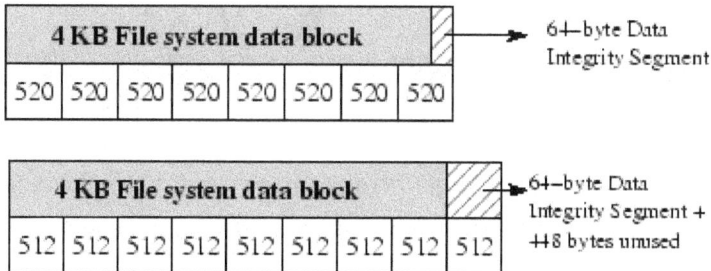

4 KB File system data block								64–byte Data Integrity Segment
520	520	520	520	520	520	520	520	

4 KB File system data block									64–byte Data Integrity Segment + 448 bytes unused
512	512	512	512	512	512	512	512	512	

(c) Structure of the data integrity segment (DIS)

Checksum of data block
Identity of data block
. . . .
Checksum of DIS

Corruption Class	Possible Causes	Detection Mechanism	Detection Operation
Checksum mismatch	Bit-level corruption; torn write; misdirected write	RAID block checksum	Any disk read
Identity discrepancy	Lost or misdirected write	File system-level block identity	File system read
Parity inconsistency	Memory corruption; lost write; bad parity calculation	RAID parity mismatch	Data scrub

Table 1: Data Integrity Segment.

The figure shows the different on-disk formats used to store the data integrity segment of a disk block on (a) enterprise class drives with 520B sectors, and on (b) near-line drives with 512B sectors. The figure also shows (c) the structure of the data integrity segment. In addition to the checksum and identity information, this structure also contains a checksum of itself.

The system, like other commercial storage systems, handles a wide range of disk-related errors. The data-integrity checks in place detect and recover from corruption errors so that they are not propagated to the user. The system does not knowingly propagate corrupt data to the user under any circumstance.

We focus on techniques used to detect silent data corruption —corruptions not detected by the disk drive or any other hardware component. Therefore, we do not describe techniques used for other errors, such as transport corruptions reported as SCSI transport errors or latent sector errors. Latent sector errors are caused by physical problems within the disk drive such as media scratches, "high-fly'" writes, etc., and detected by the disk drive itself by its inability to read or write sectors, or through its error-correction codes (ECC.) To detect silent data corruptions, the system stores extra information to disk blocks. It also periodically reads all disk blocks to perform data integrity checks. We now describe these techniques.

Data Integrity Segment

To detect disk block corruptions, the system writes a 64-byte data integrity segment along with each disk block. Figure 1 shows two techniques for storing this extra information and describes its structure. For enterprise class disks, the system uses 520-byte sectors. Thus, a 4-KB file system block is stored along with a 64-byte data-integrity segment in eight 520-byte sectors. For near-line disks, the systems use the default 512-byte sectors and store the data integrity segment for each set of eight sectors in the following sector. The protection afforded by the data integrity segments is well worth the extra space needed to store them.

One component of the data integrity segment is a checksum of the entire 4 KB file system block. The checksum is validated by the RAID layer whenever the data is read. Once a corruption has been detected, the original block can usually be restored through RAID reconstruction. We refer to corruptions detected by RAID-level checksum validation as *checksum mismatches*.

A second component of the data integrity segment is block identity information. Here, the fact that the file system is part of the storage system is utilized. The identity is the disk block's identity within the file system (e.g., this block belongs to node 5 at offset 100.) This identity is cross-checked at file read time to ensure that the block being read belongs to the file being accessed. If upon file read, the identity does not match, the data is reconstructed from parity. We refer to corruptions not detected by checksums but detected through file system identity validation as *identity discrepancies*.

Data Scrubbing

In order to pro-actively detect errors, the RAID layer periodically *scrubs* all disks. A data scrub issues read operations for each physical disk block, computes a checksum over its data, and compares the computed checksum to the checksum in its data integrity segment. If the checksum comparison fails (i.e., a checksum mismatch), the data is reconstructed from other disks in the RAID group, after those checksums are also verified. If no reconstruction is necessary, the parity of the data blocks is generated and compared with the parity stored in the parity block. If the parity does not match the verified data, the scrub process fixes the parity by regenerating it from the data blocks. In a system protected by double parity, it is possible to definitively tell which of the parity or data blocks is corrupt.

We refer to a mismatch between data and parity as *parity inconsistencies*. Note that data scrubs cannot validate the extra file-system identity information stored in the data integrity segment, since this information only has meaning to the file system and not the RAID-level scrub. Depending on system load, data scrubs are initiated on Sunday evenings. From our data, an entire RAID group is scrubbed approximately once every two weeks on average. However, we cannot ascertain from the data that every disk in the study has been scrubbed.

3. Corruption Classes

This study focuses on disk block corruptions caused by both hardware and software errors. Hardware bugs include bugs in the disk drive or the disk shelf firmware, bad memory, and adapter failures. Software bugs could also cause some corruption. Often, the cause of corruption cannot be identified. We detect different forms of corruption using the different data protection mechanisms in place. We distinguish between these forms in our study. Table 1 gives a summary of these corruption classes.

- *Checksum mismatches (CMs)*: This corruption class refers to cases where corruption is detected from mismatched data and checksum. The cause could be (i) data content corrupted by components within the data path, or (ii) a torn write, wherein only a portion of the data block is written successfully, or (iii) a misdirected write, wherein the data is written to either the wrong disk or the wrong location on the disk, thus overwriting and corrupting data. Checksum mismatches can be detected any time a disk block is read (file system reads, data scrubs, RAID reconstruction, and so on.)

- *Identity discrepancies (IDs)*: This corruption class refers to a mismatch detected when a disk block identity check is performed during a file system read. The cause could be (i) a lost write, which typically occurs because a write destined for the disk is not written. or (ii) a misdirected write, where the original disk location is not updated. We know of actual cases when the disk firmware replied successfully to a write that was never written to stable media. Identity discrepancies can be detected only during file system reads.

- *Parity inconsistencies (PIs)*: This corruption class refers to a mismatch between the parity computed from data blocks and the parity stored on disk, despite the individual checksums being valid. This error could be caused by lost or misdirected writes, in-memory corruptions, processor miscalculations, and software bugs. Parity inconsistencies are detected only during data scrubs.

Our study primarily focuses on checksum mismatches, since we find these corruptions occur much more frequently.

4.Terms

Disk class: **Enterprise Class or nearline disk drives with respectively fiber Channel and ATA interfaces.**

Disk family: A particular disk drive product. The same product (and hence a disk family) may be offered in different capacities. Typically, disks in the same family only differ in the number of platters and/or read/write heads.

Disk model: The combination of a disk family and a particular disk size. Note this term does not imply an analytical or simulation model.

Disk age: The time a disk has been in the field since its ship date, rather than the manufacture date. In practice, these two values are typically within a month of each other.

Corrupt block: This term refers to a 4-KB file system block with a checksum mismatch.

Corrupt disk: This term is used to refer to a disk drive that has at least one corrupt block.

Data collection: The storage system has a built-in, low-overhead mechanism called Auto-support to log important system events back to a central repository. These messages can be enabled for a variety of system events, including disk errors. Not all customers enable logging, although a large percentage does. Those that do, sometimes do so only after some period of initial use. These logs allow customized support based on observed events. Although these logs are primarily intended for support, they have also been utilized for analyzing various disk errors. Besides our corruption study, this repository (the ``Network Appliance Auto-support Database'') has been used in studies of disk failure and latent sector error.

Analysis: We studied corruption instances logged in tens of thousands of storage systems for a period of 41 months starting in January 2004. These systems belong to a range of different models, run different versions of storage-controller software (perhaps with one or more updates during the study period), and contain many models or versions of hardware components. To have a complete history of the activities of the disks used in the study, we constrained our sample to only those disks shipped after January 2004. Our sample consisted of 153 million disk drives. These drives belong to 14 disk families and 31 distinct models.

To derive statistically significant results, we often further constrain the sample set depending on the analysis being performed. For example, we sometimes use shorter time periods for our analysis to maximize the number of models we can study; clearly not all disk families and models have been in the field for the same duration. The disk models we consider for each study may have one of these constraints:

- Model has at least 1000 disks in the field for time period being considered.
- Model has at least 1000 disks in the field and at least 15 corrupt disks for time being considered.

The first constraint is used for studies of factors that impact checksum mismatches, while other studies use the second constraint. Besides the constraints on the model sample, we often restrict our data to include only the first 17 months since a drive was shipped. This helps make results more comparable, since many drives in the study were shipped on different dates and have been in the field for different amounts of time.

While we usually present data for individual disk models, we sometimes also report averages (mean values) for near-line disks and enterprise class disks. Since the sample size for different disk models per disk class varies considerably, we weigh the average by the sample size of each disk model in the respective class.

5. Other Data Corruptions

This section presents our results on the frequency of occurrence for two corruption classes: identity discrepancies and parity inconsistencies. These corruption classes are further described below.

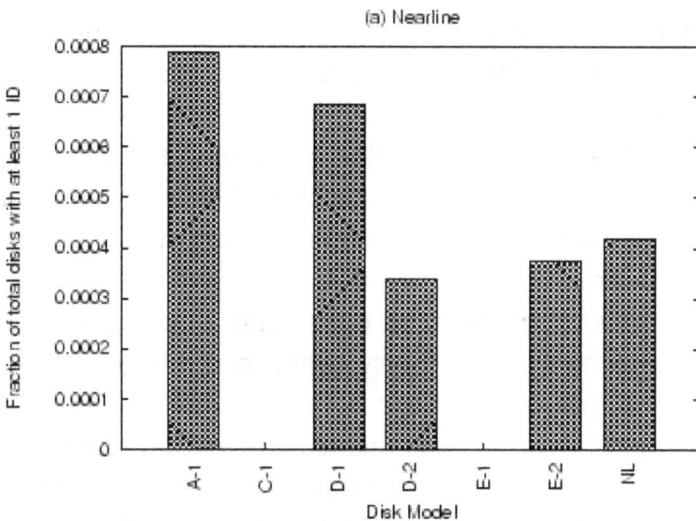

Figure 5. Graph showing frequency in corruption occurrences

Identity Discrepancies

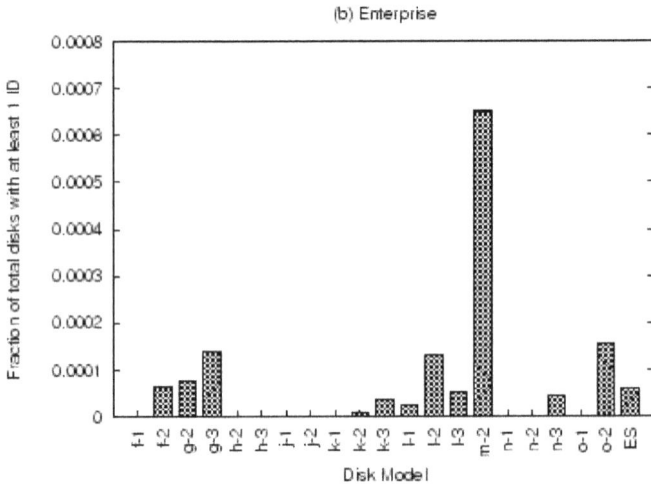

(b) Enterprise

Figure 6. Identity Discrepancies. The figures show the fraction of disks with at least one identity discrepancy within 17 months of shipping to the field for (a) near-line disk models, and (b) enterprise class disk models.

These errors were detected in 365 out of the 1.53 million disks. Figure 10 presents the fraction of disks of each disk model that developed identity discrepancies in the 17 months under scrutiny. We see that the fraction is more than an order of magnitude lower than that for checksum mismatches for both near-line and enterprise class disks.

Since the fraction of disks that develop identity discrepancies is low, the system recommends replacement of the disk once the first identity discrepancy is detected. Note, that even though the number of identity discrepancies is small, silent data corruption would have occurred if not for the validation of the stored contextual file system information.

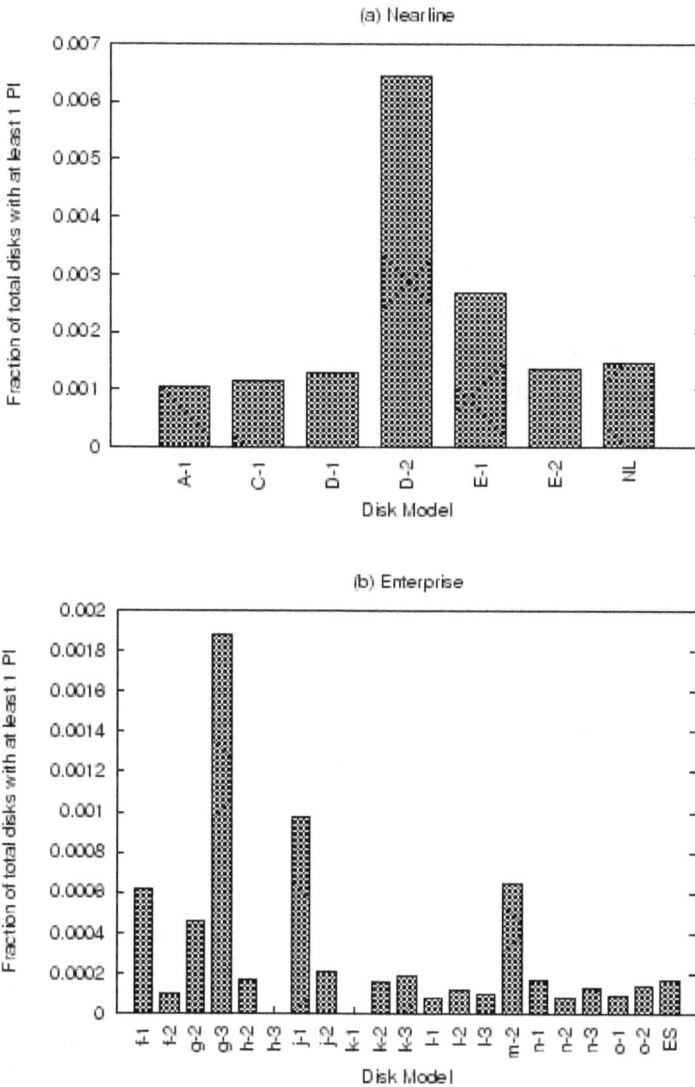

Figure 7. Parity Inconsistencies. The figures show the fraction of disks with at least one parity inconsistency within 17 months of shipping to the field for (a) near-line disk models, and (b) enterprise class disk models.

Parity Inconsistencies

These errors are detected by data scrubbing. In the absence of a second parity disk, one cannot identify which disk is at fault. Therefore, to prevent potential data loss on disk failure, the system fixes the inconsistency by rewriting parity. This scenario further motivates double-parity protection schemes.

Figure 11 presents the fraction of disks of each disk model that caused parity inconsistencies within 17 months since ship date. The fraction is 4.4 times lower than that for checksum mismatches with near-line disks and about 3.5 times lower than that for checksum mismatches for enterprise class disks.

These results assume that the parity disk is at fault. Counting the number of incorrect parity disks reflects the actual number of errored disks, since: (i) entire shelves of disks are typically of the same age and same model, and (ii) the incidence of these inconsistencies is low, hence, it is unlikely that multiple different disks in the same RAID group would be at fault.

(6) RELIGION AND CORRUPTION

The world is becoming a more dangerous place with the loss of shared values, the rise of unpredictable leaders, the increasing concentration of wealth and power, the rejection of science, logic, expertise, and even truth, increasing xenophobia and polarization, a disregard for the needs and desires of the young and of future generations, the headlong destruction of environmental resources and life-support systems, the destabilization of the climate, and a debt-driven economic and financial system raping the planet for short-term profit. These contrary winds are sweeping away many hopeful signs of progress from the past, and seem to be leading us to a catastrophe of multiple dimensions and unimaginable consequences. The parallel with the 1930s is frightening.

1. Corruption

I was asked to reflect on the moral dimensions of corruption, particularly in the light of recent political events. Corruption is traditionally defined as the abuse of public office for private gain, including bribery, nepotism and misappropriation; extra-legal efforts by individuals or groups to gain influence over the actions of the bureaucracy; the collusion between parties in the public and private sectors to benefit the latter; and more generally, influencing the shaping of policies and institutions in ways that benefit the contributing private parties at the expense of the broader public welfare (Lopez-Claros, 2015.) Upon reflection, it seems the corruption eating into the vitals of global society today is more than just the material corruption of bribery for personal gain. It is any undue preference given to personal or private gain at the expense of the public or collective interest, including the betrayal of a public trust or office in government, the manipulation of corporate responsibility for the purpose of self-enrichment, the distortion of truth and denial of science to manipulate the public for ideological ends, and even the misuse of religion to acquire power and wealth. Corruption is just one expression of priority given to one's self over others, of egoism over altruism, of personal over collective benefit.

The impact of corruption in terms of environmental destruction and mismanagement is often underestimated, but it is a principal behind the failure of many efforts at environmental protection and management, whether they be addressing trafficking in endangered species, illegal logging and fishing, or ignoring or evading environmental regulations.

For me, as a systems scientist, there must be a simple underlying explanation for this. Like the struggle between good and evil, it is nothing new, but it is expressed in complex new forms.

2. Morality

It starts with humans. We are born with an animal nature but the potential for much more, a potential realized through education, an education with material, intellectual and ethical/moral/spiritual dimensions. Without the right education, our ego and selfish desires dominate, and our life is driven by self-interest and physical passions. It is natural to be selfish and aggressive, and for many, "you can't change human nature." Corruption expresses this, in forms such as war, crime, dictatorships, and the many other ways that self-interest is expressed in today's world. Every civilization in which these forces of disintegration became dominant eventually collapsed.

Self-centeredness in all its forms has become the ideology for self-justification, whether in the neoliberal economy that drives the concentration of wealth and power, political ideologies of total individual freedom that reject any constraints or regulations in the common interest, national sovereignty that leans to isolationism and self-protection behind strong borders, xenophobia that places one ethnicity or culture above all others, multinational corporations for which the right to profits overrides all other interests, or criminal syndicates for which illegal activities are the fastest route to money and power. These ideologies forget that Adam Smith's invisible hand of self-interest was balanced by an individual sense of moral responsibility and assume that the larger good will somehow "naturally" emerge or trickle down from all these selfish drives.

The irony is that humans have the capacity for so much more, as the history of the rise of civilizations has repeatedly demonstrated. Education allows culture, science, innovation, and social cohesion to develop. It cultivates the potentials available in each individual, whether the physical capacity for athletic performance or feats of endurance, the intellectual capacity for rational thought, scientific investigation, and cultural creation, the emotional capacity for altruism, empathy, solidarity, and cooperation, or the spiritual capacity for love, humility, forgiveness, volition, generosity, and self-effacement into a higher collective entity. These dimensions of education are complementary and mutually reinforcing; neglecting any of them can lead to undesirable outcomes.

Fundamental to this is the shared morality on which any society must be built, with values that contribute to social cohesion, that favor unity in diversity and leaving no one behind. Education transmits those values and ensures the sustainability of society. Today, those values are receding. The Baha'i international governing body, the Universal House of Justice, has so well described "the multiplying ills of a disordered society. Over the last year, it has become clearer still that, in different nations in different ways, the social consensus around ideals that have traditionally united and bound together a people is increasingly worn and spent. It can no longer offer a reliable defense against a variety of self-serving, intolerant, and toxic ideologies that feed upon discontent and resentment. With a conflicted world appearing every day less sure of itself, the proponents of these destructive doctrines grow bold and brazen. We recall the unequivocal verdict from the Supreme Pen [Baha'u'llah]: "They hasten forward to Hell Fire and mistake it for light.

Well-meaning leaders of nations and people of goodwill are left struggling to repair the fractures evident in society and powerless to prevent their spread. The effects of all these are not only to be seen in outright conflict or a collapse in order. In the distrust that pits neighbor against neighbor and severs family ties, in the antagonism of so much of what passes for social discourse, in the casualness with which appeals to ignoble human motivations are used to win power and pile up riches; in all these lie unmistakable signs that the moral force which sustains society has become gravely depleted." (UHJ 2015, §2)

Many people today, particularly intellectuals, the young, and those from cultures that retain a sense of collective purpose, still hold to these values and despair at the destructive forces swirling around them, but the faltering or failure of many of the more liberal movements of the left shows that an intellectual attachment to human rights, solidarity, concern for the excluded and marginalized, and redistribution of wealth is not sufficient. Movements of the left are just as driven by ego, ambition, and the struggle for power as those on the right.

What is missing is the level of spiritual education and transformation in each individual. Human potential comes to fruition when cultivated in a spirit of selfless service, without pride, with no desire to be seen as superior to anyone else, and a readiness to accompany others in their own acts of service and thus to become part of an organically-evolving learning community. This dimension of education is largely absent today in societies around the world. Spiritual education empowers every individual to refine their character and to contribute to an ever-advancing civilization. At this level, effective responsibility and accountability can be built into the institutions of society (Dahl, 2015.)

3. Religion

This leads us to the great absence of a primary tool to address the crises in today's world: religion. Traditionally, religion has provided the multitudes with basic moral and ethical values. Religion has taught about good and evil, saints and sinners, and the good values that build a society, versus the greed, lust, indolence, pride, and violence valued in today's market society. Yet today, even in societies that claim to be religious, those ethical values are largely lacking or are merely given lip service while the great majority pursues self-centered, materialistic objectives. Where religion has been replaced by a secular ideology, the results are no better, and fear may enforce common values rather than the positive internal motivation that religion can provide.

Interestingly, a recent study of civilization-building by an avowed atheist has identified religion as the main explanation for the rise of complex, large-scale civilizations (Turchin, 2016.) The same researcher warned of the impending collapse of our civilization because of the increasing concentration of wealth, loss of social cohesion, and abandonment of the young (Turchin, 2010.)

However, religion in most of its expressions today is not up to the task. In its statement to the World Summit on Sustainable Development in Johannesburg in 2002, the Bahá'í International Community analyzed the challenge facing religions regarding international efforts at the United Nations to address world problems. It highlighted "both the constructive role that religion can play in creating a peaceful and prosperous global order, and the destructive impact that religious fanaticism can have on the stability and progress of the world," and referred to the UN failure "to address religious bigotry as a major obstacle to peace and well-being.

"It is becoming increasingly clear that passage to the culminating stage in the millennia-long process of the organization of the planet as one home for the entire human family cannot be accomplished in a spiritual vacuum. Religion, the Bahá'í Scriptures aver, "is the source of illumination, the cause of development, and the animating impulse of all human advancement" and "has been the basis of all civilization and progress in the history of mankind." It is the source of meaning and hope for the vast majority of the planet's inhabitants, and it has a limitless power to inspire sacrifice, change, and long-term commitment in its followers. It is inconceivable that a peaceful and prosperous global society – a society which nourishes a spectacular diversity of cultures and nations – can be established and sustained without directly and substantively involving the world's great religions in its design and support.

At the same time, it cannot be denied that the power of religion has also been perverted to turn neighbor against neighbor. The Bahá'í Scriptures state that "religion must be the source of fellowship, the cause of unity and the nearness of God to man. If it rouses hatred and strife, it is evident that the absence of religion is preferable, and an irreligious man is better than one who professes it." So long as religious animosities can destabilize the world, it will be impossible to foster a global pattern of sustainable development."

Given the record of religious fanaticism, it is understandable that the United Nations has been hesitant to invite religion into its negotiations. However, the UN can no longer afford to ignore the immeasurable good that religions have done and continue to do in the world, or the salubrious, far-reaching contributions that they can make to the establishment of a peaceful, prosperous and sustainable global order. Indeed, the United Nations will only succeed in establishing such a global order to the extent that it taps into the power and vision of religion. To do so will require accepting religion not merely as a vehicle for the delivery and execution of development initiatives, but as an active partner in the conceptualization, design, implementation and evaluation of global policies and programs. The historically justified wall separating the United Nations and religions must fall to the imperatives of a world struggling toward unity and justice.

The real onus, however, is on the religions themselves. Religious followers and, more importantly, religious leaders must show that they are worthy partners in the great mission of building a sustainable world civilization. To do so will require that religious leaders work conscientiously and untiringly to exorcise religious bigotry and superstition from within their faith traditions. It will necessitate that they embrace freedom of conscience for all people, including their followers, and renounce claims to religious exclusivity and finality.

"…until the religions of the world renounce fanaticism and work whole-heartedly to eliminate it from within their ranks, peace and prosperity will prove chimerical." Indeed, the responsibility for the plight of humanity rests, in large part, with the world's religious leaders. It is they who must raise their voices to end the hatred, exclusivity, oppression of conscience, violations of human rights, denial of equality, opposition to science, and glorification of materialism, violence. and terrorism, which are perpetrated in the name of religious truth. Moreover, it is the followers of all religions who must transform their own lives and take up the mantle of sacrifice for and service to the well-being of others, and thus contribute to the realization of the long-promised reign of peace and justice on earth." (BIC, 2002)

There are a few steps in that direction, such as the encyclical of Pope Francis (2015), but most of the world is still not listening, especially those who have long since rejected religion as pertaining to the modern world.

In its message to leaders of religion, the Universal House of Justice referred explicitly to corruption within religions. "Among the many temptations the world offers, the test that has, not surprisingly, preoccupied religious leaders is that of exercising power in matters of belief.

No one who has dedicated long years to earnest meditation and study of the scriptures of one or another of the great religions requires any further reminder of the oft-repeated axiom regarding the potentiality of power to corrupt, and to do so increasingly as such power grows. The unheralded inner victories won in this respect by unnumbered clerics all down through the ages have no doubt been one of the chief sources of organized religion's creative strength and must rank as one of its highest distinctions. To the same degree, surrender to the lure of worldly power and advantage, on the part of other religious leaders, has cultivated a fertile breeding ground for cynicism, corruption, and despair among all who observe it. The implications for the ability of religious leadership to fulfill its social responsibility at this point in history need no elaboration.

With every day that passes, the danger grows that the rising fires of religious prejudice will ignite a worldwide conflagration, the consequences of which are unthinkable. Such a danger civil government, unaided, cannot overcome. Nor should we delude ourselves that appeals for mutual tolerance can alone hope to extinguish animosities that claim to possess Divine sanction. The crisis calls on religious leadership for a break with the past as decisive as those that opened the way for society to address equally corrosive prejudices of race, gender, and nation. Whatever justification exists for exercising influence in matters of conscience lies in serving the well-being of humankind. At this greatest turning point in the history of civilization, the demands of such a service could not be clearer. 'The well-being of mankind, its peace, and security are unattainable,' Baha'u'llah urges, 'unless and until its unity is firmly established.' " (UHJ 2002)

The different propensity to corruption observed in different countries has been explained in comparative politics by, among other variables, the specific national values, whether they be crystallized in religion, family orientation, or confidence in the state. In such a perspective, as Pareto notices, "the differences [between countries] are to be found in the substance, that is, in the sentiment of the people; where they are more (or less) honest, there we find a more (or less) honest government" (Pareto, 1916, 625.) Elster, too, emphasizes the relevance of moral costs: "Although it is hard to prove, I believe that the variation in corruption across countries is explained largely by the degree of public-spiritedness of their officials, not by the cleverness of institutional design" (Elster, 1989c, 158.) And Mény observes that "Corruption is thus more likely to spread in cases where the 'immune defense systems' of the group tend to weaken and the 'moral cost' drops, as will occur when public behavior is less prized than private, when producing results comes to matter more than observing standards, monetary values more than ethical or symbolic values" (2000, 213.) Especially in cross-national comparison, the general issue of values (in particular, but not only, political values), that help the spreading of corruption, has been discussed.

Variations in the moral costs can explain the different individual responses to similar opportunities for corruption: "People in a given society face the same institutions but may have different values" (Elster, 1989a, 39.) Given similar institutional conditions, the levels of political corruption will vary with the average moral attitudes among the citizens and the public administrators. Looking for cultural traditions, norms, and values which influence the activities and choices of individuals belonging to different societies and organizations, a first observation, fueled initially by comparison between European countries, points at *religion*. Case studies seemed to indicate that protestant countries have higher ethical standards, while corruption seems more widespread in Catholic countries, and in particular, Southern Europe. From case studies and small comparisons, the analysis of the relationship between religion and corruption has expanded to macro comparison, using different measures of corruption as a dependent variable (often the TI index) and correlating them with statistical or survey data about religiosity.

In research on 33 countries, La Porta et al. (1997, 337) found a positive correlation between hierarchical forms of religion (Catholic, Eastern Orthodox, and Muslim) and corruption; although, in another research study on 114 countries, that correlation weakens significantly if controlled for GDP per head (La Porta et al., 1999, 251-2.) Similar results are obtained in a macro-comparison where levels of corruption emerge as negatively correlated with the percentage of Protestants in the total population (Treisman, 2000, 428). Also, according to another research study (Paldam, 1999), corruption is lower in countries with a large faction of Reform Christianity and Tribal religion, and higher in countries with a large influence of Pre-Reform Christianity, Islam, Buddhism, and Hinduism, with particular and significant impact for Reform Protestants and Anglicans. Catholicism has been mentioned as facilitating hierarchical relationships (because of the role the clergy acquires as a mediator between humans and the God while presenting the possibility, via confession, to be absolved of guilt and guilty feelings).

While the protestant, Weberian "spirit of capitalism" develops individual responsibility, the Catholic religion socializes to the possibility of buying pardon, via the formal act of contrition, including material payments. In both Italy and Spain, the intertwining of spiritual and material powers has a long tradition in the functioning of the clergy as brokers within a clientelist machine where the sponsorship of the local priest helped finding not only absolution, but also material rewards, such as job or housing (Allum, 1995.) In Italy, this link between corruption and religious behavior is epitomized by the Neapolitan politician and former Minister Cirino Pomicino who, to thank good God for the success of his surgery, asked the entrepreneur Francesco Zecchina (with whom he was in illicit business), to give money to a Catholic charity: "He asked me for a contribution of 100 million lira −10 million at Christmas and 10 at Eastern, for five years− to the priest Salvatore D'Angelo for the 'Village of the Child' in Maddaloni. He made this request when he came back from Houston, where he had had a heart surgery operation in 1984-5, specifying that he had made the vow of helping those boys. (...) I objected that it seemed strange to me I had to pay for his votive offering, but he replied that I had to pay" (CD, n. 344, 6/5/1993, p. 4.) Research on Mafia bosses has also stressed the particular role that religion played, not only for a long time in terms of legitimation of their power, but also in developing their self-images as "fair men," deferent to God and the family.

Personal responsibility for sin in the Protestant culture is counterposed to the institutional forgiveness of the Catholic church: "Protestant cultures are less understanding towards lapses from grace and press more urgently to institutionalize virtue and cast out the wicked" (Treisman, 2000, 427.) Protestant societies have more pronounced separation between the state and the church, a more vivacious civil society, and more tolerance for challenges to authority and individual dissent than Catholicism or Islam (Treisman, 2000, 427-428.) Edward Banfield (1956), in his research on "amoral familism" in the Southern Italian village of Montegrano, observed that some values and norms affect the political capacity of a community to pursue public goods. According to him, widespread poverty was linked with amoral familism, which is the lack of capacity to act in the name of a collective good that goes beyond the immediate, material interest of the nuclear family (Banfield, 1956, 10.) Amoral familyism interacts with the political behavior in so far as nobody will pursue the interest of the community (ibidem, 83-4), and the citizens will believe that all those in power are self-interested and corrupt (ibidem, 99.) In a sort of self-fulfilling prophecy, the amoral familyist in a public administration will accept bribes when he does not fear punishment, and all the members of the society will assume that he is corrupt anyhow (ibidem, 92.)

Family ties emerged in investigations on corruption as factors often providing the strong bond of solidarity needed for risky activities. For instance, in relation to Sicily, Michele Pantaleoni has noted that "It is significant that of 18 entrepreneurs in public works ... two are the direct relations of parliamentarians, three married to the children of national-level party leaders, one the son of the director of a regional assessorate, another the son of the president of a public body." (Pantaleoni 1984, 184.) Often, corrupt deals have been justified with the necessity of finding support for an elderly mother or many growing children. Relatives offer a cover, in terms of material affairs, but also psychological support and justification of "minor misdemeanors" in the name of superior values. A functionary, for example, justified his attempt to collect bribes by selling information on questions in a television quiz-show, with the needs of his mother: "I did it because I wanted, but I also didn't want...My mother has heart disease, and a monthly pension of only 600.000 lira" ("La Republica", 17/4/1997, p. 21.)

Research on different countries indicated a strong link between political corruption and *patrimonialism*. In the studies dealing with corruption in Third World countries, corruption has been linked to their patrimonial character defined as "not simply to the persistence in social relationships generally of personality principles of kinship, clanship, and client-ship, but, more crucially, to their inevitable invocation in dealing with

the state" (Theobald, 1996, 13.) In Spain, where political corruption became in the nineties "the single most
salient issue in Spanish politics" (Heywood, 1995, 726;
see also Pérez-Diaz, 1996), commentators explained
its development with the traditional emphasis on
amiguismo, involving the use of brokers in the relationships with the public administration (Heywood, 1997,
70-71.) Studies of corruption in Portugal recalled the
long-lasting presence of *caciques,* "influential local
bosses such as priests, lawyers and others who were
able to offer to the government in power bundles of
votes from their local community" (Magone, 1996, 9.)

The survival of corruption even after democratization
has been explained with the presence of a "soft state,"
i.e., "a state that fails to supersede personal, family,
ethnic, and tribal loyalties. Many elected presidents or
democratically appointed officers do not perceive the
boundaries between state and private finances. This
'soft state' is perpetuated in new democracies because
political institutions are usually very weak" (Pinheiro,
1994, 38.)

Many political scandals emerged in Greece under
the so-called "patrimonial socialism" led by Andreas
Papandreou (ibid.)

As for Japan, another country in which corruption
appears to be widespread, a persistent weakness of the
concept of public good that only lately and imperfectly
was distinguished from that of the private good of
those in power (Bouissou, 1997) has often been cited.

Corruption in the former French colonies in Africa
was facilitated by developing personalized relationships
between the African leaders and their counterpart

in France (Médard, 1997.) In Italy, the power of the former national secretary of the Socialist Party, Bettino Craxi, was an example of *caciquism* (Sapelli, 1994.) In similar research, the Italian political culture emerges as alienated, fragmented, and particularistic, with low trust in politics and public administration (Almond and Verba, 1963.)

More recently, Robert Putnam (1993) developed similar hypotheses to explain institutional output. According to his influential research, when civic values are widespread, politics is perceived as oriented to the public good, and politicians and citizens behave. In civic regions, citizens trust their politicians to be honest, and politicians meet high moral standards; vice versa, in uncivil regions, citizens and politicians consider corruption the norm (ibidem, 135.)

Macro-comparison indicated that trust (as measured by the World Value Survey) has a significant negative impact on corruption, even controlling for GDP per head (La Porta et al., 1997: 336.) Similarly, Husted (1999) discovered that acceptance of inequalities is correlated with corruption. Civic-ness is also linked with respect for the law; that is, the internalization of the conception of a *Rechtstaat*. Alessandro Pizzorno (1992, 66-68) focused on developing public ethics, distinguishing between a political ethic (sense of politics) and a state ethic (sense of the state.) The political ethic refers to collectivities that do not coincide with the state territory (classes, ethnic, or religious groups, etc.) Those who have a "sense of the state" instead perceive institutions as oriented towards the public good of the community defined within state borders. In Italy, loyalty to the two large communities –the socialist one and the catholic one– prevailed over loyalty to the state, jeopardizing the development of a sense of respect for the Law of the State.

Since the seventies, the "sense of politics" has diminished, with the weakening of the moral constraints against corruption. As Michael Johnston observed, the very notion of corruption is related to "the rise of a *'system of public order'*: a relatively durable framework of social and legal standards defining practical limits of behavior by holders of government roles, and by those who seek to influence them" (Johnston, 1994, 11.) If this system is not implemented or internalized, corruption can develop. Corruption spreads when corrupt behaviors are not stigmatized by the elite and/or the public opinion, becoming "white" or "gray" forms of corruption (1970.)

Many cultural explanations employed as the explanation of corruption in terms of values, have been accused of describing more than accounting for. As Paul Heywood (1997, 70) mentioned, "One of the most familiar, yet also one of the most easily dismissed, explanations of political corruption in Spain is one which relies on some notion of 'national character'... Just as Germans are supposedly efficient, and the French stylish, so Spaniards are lazy and corrupt."

The open question is, first, why should an immoral society produce a corrupt political class? The response that the political class is usually selected from within that population is not satisfactory since it is well known that specific positions/professions involve specific paths of socialization.

A parallel explanation could be that, in an amoral society, politicians need not fear stigmatization (and electoral withdrawal) if they are caught in corrupt acts. Here, however, Italian and Spanish history (as well as the vicissitudes of many regime crises in Southern countries) indicate that scandals do emerge and produce strong emotional (and concrete) effects in societies characterized by weak civic-ness. As Benfield observed, in a society of amoral familyists, law-and-order sentiments are widespread (1956, 93.) Looking more in-depth into the interaction of corruption dynamics and widespread values, it was observed that lack of trust indeed interacts with the spread of corruption, especially since in such societies citizens (and entrepreneurs) are pushed to "buy" the public services they do not think they could obtain otherwise. At its turn, corruption confirms the appropriateness of that mistrust, fueling it even more. "Gifts," "favors," and "expressions of solidarity" are considered "innocent" behavior if third parties are not directly harmed. In a culture characterized by a positive evaluation of gift, bribes are often masked as an innocuous gift. As the Italian broker Zampini explained, a sort of escalation in this strategy of gift can be a way of testing the moral barriers of the potential partners and slowly socializing him to illegality. Zampini's networking was also furthered through his organization of "foreign junkets," an innovation for which he claims authorship: "The money flowed briskly. Once on the plane, Concorde I think, I spent 3 million on presents for everybody. I remember I asked Giuseppe Gatti [leader of the DC group on the city council] to draw up the bill, and he was astonished by the amount. But he didn't say anything, and as far as I was concerned, from then on, he was "done," compromised, prepared to come in on the game." (*L' Espresso*, 18/11/1984, p. 45.)

For entrepreneurs, the decision to pay or not pay a bribe depends on the entrepreneur's "moral propensity" to illegal behavior. The condition of illegality may cause an "emotional suffering" which can influence that choice, even considering it as the result of rational calculation. To explain his final rebellion, an entrepreneur from Bari who had paid bribes for fifteen years declared: "I couldn't look at myself in the mirror anymore. I felt completely shitty. It seemed wrong, humiliating" (*L' Espresso*, 18/11/1984, p. 34.) And, paying bribes is often "neutralized" as normal behavior, as an Italian entrepreneur declared. "My colleagues also told me that that was the way things worked, that everyone did it and at bottom, there was nothing strange about it" (*L' Espresso*, 18/11/1984, p. 41); "It was a sort of custom. ... Since that was the system, more or less, I preferred to be part of the system" (*Panorama*, 14/2/1993, p. 61.)

Moreover, mechanisms exist inside firms for a progressive and painless initiation into the rituals and institutional obligations of corruption. Enso Papi recalled that when he was nominated manager of the Cogefar, a company controlled by FIAT, he was given "a booklet where all the 'obligations' and payment dates of the company were recorded. A list of names and sums; an inheritance which had to be respected to the letter. *Illegality was so regularized that I didn't feel I was perpetrating a criminal act*" (*Panorama*, 16/4/1994, p. 86, emphasis added.) Thus, each manager ends up considering their individual contribution to the complex operation underlying an act of corruption as part of a decision-making process which lies outside their personal responsibility.

Similarly, skills and knowledge in corruption practices are passed on, in numerous family-run businesses, directly from father to son: "I paid my first bribe in 1966 when I inherited this enterprise from my daddy. We paid for 45 years, since when the Republican Army was founded" stated an entrepreneur who has been arrested in relation to ferreting supplies to the army (*La Repubblica*, 25/10/1995, p. 9.)

Corruption is also often justified in the name of a superior goal. Several politicians involved in recent corruption investigations stressed their *"efficient image"* of a public administrator, a self-representation which offers a "moral" justification of corruption. The description given of an eminent colleague by a Calabrian administrator makes the point nicely: "He really is convinced that he always pursued the general interest with abnegation and public spirit. Securing investment, even though corruption served the interest of the population and contributed to the prosperity of the city. Paris was worth a mass, and public works were worth a bit of bribery even if by doing so the system was perpetuated. He said: "That's the way it is. Otherwise, we have no public works, no employment, and no help for the less well-off.'" (Licandro and Varano 1993, 71.)

Similarly, for entrepreneurs the moral costs of breaking the law are attenuated by what one of them defines as the "ethic of responsibility an entrepreneur has towards his firm and its employees" (*L' Espresso*,

21/6/1992, p. 31) and another as "the interests of the
thousands of employees and shareholders to whom I
felt I owed paramount responsibility" (*La Repubblica*,
18/5/1993, p. 5) or the responsibility "for keeping a firm
with a thousand employees going" (PRIM, p. 15.) Like
other "white-collar crimes", corruption is an illegal act
closely connected to activities which are both legal and
considered socially positive (Solivetti, 1987, 71.) This
is true when the firms involved in corruption, as often
happened in Italy, were specialized in satisfying public
demand, thus reducing their opportunities of working in
the private sector. The particular location of their plant,
the specific skills they had developed in a learning-by-
doing fashion, or the discrete investments made at the
behest of the public customer rendered them particularly susceptible to bribery demands (Williamson 1989,
143.) One of the Pio Albergo Trivulzio' s contractors
stated: "Giving these people money wasn't a result of
free choice. Having equipped the firm with sophisticated and expensive machinery and taken on a large
number of highly specialized employees, the firm's
survival depends on getting contracts" (TM, p. 30.)

The only solution to the multiple challenges threatening us today is to reinforce the spiritual founda-
tions of society, and to help every willing individual to
begin the process of internal transformation, and each
community to launch itself on a collective process of
responsibility and transformation. Only in this way can
we rebuild, from the bottom up, solid ethical founda-
tions for the world society that must ultimately emerge
from this age of frustration and transition.

(7) CORRUPTION AND CULTURE

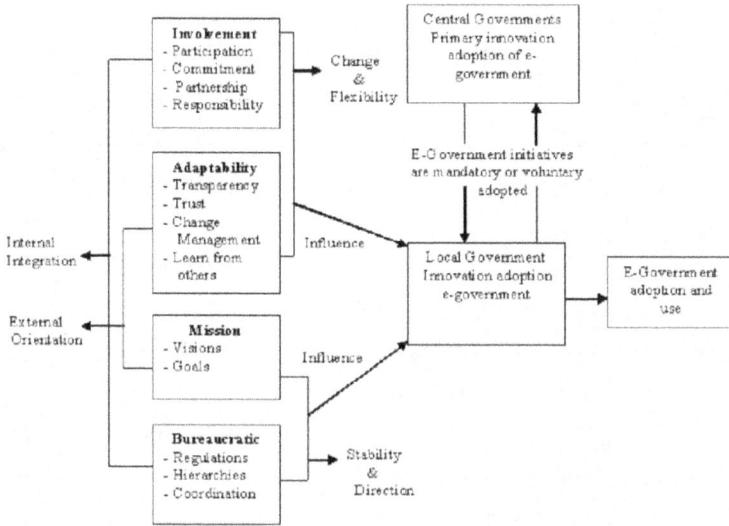

Figure 8. Variables of cultural corruption

The world is shrinking, but its cultures remain worlds apart, as do its ethical norms. Bribery, kickbacks, cronyism, and nepotism seem more prevalent in some parts of the world, and one wants to know why. Is it because some peoples are less ethical than others? Or is it because they have different ethical systems and regard these behaviors as acceptable?

The phenomenon of corruption illustrates these realities. Corruption is best understood as behavior that corrupts, undermining the cultural system in which it occurs. Because cultures can operate in vastly different ways, vastly different kinds of behavior can corrupt.

Practices that Westerners consider questionable, such as cronyism and nepotism, may be functional in other cultures. Practices that are routine and acceptable in the West, such as suing for breach of contract, may be corrupting in a wide range of cultures, Western and non-Western, but for very different reasons.

The West is Universalist in its outlook: the general consensus is that every society works, or should work, essentially the same way. Its business practices, for example, should be based on a market system characterized by transparency and regulated by laws that apply to everyone. A country that fails to conform to this model is easily labeled "underdeveloped" or "dysfunctional". It follows from this view that that corruption is basically the same in Sweden as in Sudan.

The reality, however, is that different cultures use different systems to do things. Whereas Western cultures are primarily rule-based, most of the world's cultures are relationship-based. Westerners trust the system, while people are bonded by personal honor, filial duty, friendship, or long-term mutual obligation. Loyalty to cronies is suspect behavior in the West but represents high moral character in much of the world.

What is corrupt in the West may be acceptable elsewhere. The classic example of the purchasing agent illustrates this point. The Western purchasing agent is expected to award contracts based on the quality of bids and transparency of available financial information about the bidders. An agent who favors friends is viewed as corrupt, because cronyism subverts this transparency-based system. It creates a conflict of interest; a choice good for the agent and his or her cronies may not be good for the company.

In much of the world, however, cronyism is a foundation for trust. A purchasing agent does business with friends because friends can be trusted. He or she may not even ask to see the company financials, since this could insult the other's honor. It is assumed that cronies will follow through on the deal, not because they fear a lawsuit, but because they do not wish to sacrifice a valuable relationship in an economy where relationships are the key to business. In such a system it is in the company's interest for the agent to do business with friends, and cronyism may present no conflict of interest.

What is acceptable in the West may be corrupt elsewhere. Even so basic a practice as negotiation, which is routine in the West, can disrupt harmony in Confucian cultures. Westerners organize their affairs around agreements, deals, or contracts, relying on a concept of covenant that traces back to the ancient Middle East. These agreements are hammered out in negotiation, as when labor and management sit across the table from each other. This practice is functional and constructive, so long as it proceeds according to rules of fair play and good faith.

Confucian cultures are based primarily on loyalty and obligation to friends, family, or superiors rather than on a system of rules. Before the expansion of international trade in the nineteenth and twentieth centuries, most commerce was local and followed traditional norms and ethical standards. With the expansion of international trade, however, businesses operated across cultural and linguistic boundaries. Misunderstandings and transgressions, both intended and unintended, became commonplace. To some extent, perceptions of corruption may derive from cultural differences, because behavior considered corrupt in one society may represent a normal business practice in another.

One example can be found in the Chinese concept of *guanxi*, which refers to the reciprocal obligations and benefits expected from a network of personal connections. A person with a powerful level of *guanxi* is considered a preferred business partner because such a person can utilize connections to obtain business or government approvals. *Guanxi* can derive from extended family, school friends and alumni, work colleagues, members of common clubs or organizations, and business associates. Chinese businesspeople seek to cultivate an intricate and extensive web of lifelong *guanxi* relationships. The key expectation in *guanxi* networks is reciprocity in granting favors; failing to reciprocate is considered a breach of trust. The greater the favor asked or granted, the greater the favor owed. *Guanxi* thus generates a cycle of favors. Among the questionable practices facilitated by *guanxi* are certain corrupt favoritisms such as nepotism (favoring family members) and cronyism (favoring friends.) Relatively high levels of nepotism or cronyism are accepted and tolerated in many non-Western cultures, not only in China. As applied to business transactions, *guanxi* opens doors and creates opportunities for business relationships and dealings. *Guanxi* is not corrupt. However, strong *guanxi* connections and obligations can serve as an incentive to corruption.

Many traditional business practices around the world are rooted in concepts analogous to *guanxi*, as in the practice of using business gifts or personal connections to speed up transactions both large and small. Russians use the term *blat* to refer to the ability to do things through personal networks or contacts with people of influence. The Japanese have adapted the English word *connections* to coin a term of their own, *konne*. In Pakistan, using personal *sifarish* ("recommendation") refers to the ability to contact the right official on the most favorable terms. The French expression for bribe is *pot de vin* ("jug of wine"), which implies friendly relations. In Urdu and Hindi, petty bribes are known as *chai pani* ("tea water".) In West Africa, the term is *dash*. The English colloquial term *grease* and the German *schmiergeld* ("grease money") imply lubrication or easing of resistance to the transaction. In Mozambique, one term for corruption is *cabritismo* or "goatism," which is derived from the saying "a goat eats where it is tethered."

The universality of such terms suggests that various forms of business bribery and graft are prevalent worldwide. However, specific business activities considered acceptable in some societies may be considered taboo in others. Thus, the American practice of lobbying legislators and governmental agencies would be considered an illegal form of buying influence in many other countries. In some societies, gift giving to chiefs, elders, or religious leaders is considered not only acceptable and appropriate, but even a mandatory traditional expression of respect and obligation.

A survey conducted by KPMG in the United Kingdom found that while 80 percent of respondents agreed that the UK Anti-Corruption Act attempted to address the problem of corruption, 58 percent believed that the Act was impractical and ignored the reality that bribery is an accepted way of doing business in many countries. Other similar studies have revealed widespread international criticism of U.S. anti-corruption law as hypocritical, given the American business practice of offering gifts to potential customers or clients (e.g., trips to conferences, golf outings, tickets to entertainment and sporting events, use of luxury facilities such as spas, condos, and country clubs, etc.)

(8) BRIBERY, CORRUPTION AND HIRING IN THE CORPORATE WORLD

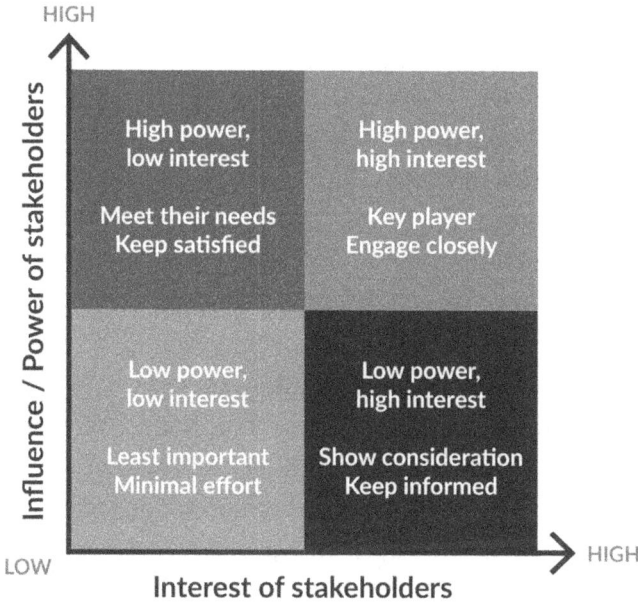

Figure 9. Hiring in the corporate world

The U.S. government has been investigating the hiring practices of U.S. businesses and has claimed that hiring relatives of government officials in exchange for government business or government action violates corruption laws. Businesses should review and revamp anti-corruption policies and hiring procedures to ensure legal and ethical hiring practices.

In August 2015, the SEC reached a settlement with BNY Mellon based on allegations that the firm gave internships to relatives of officials at a Middle Eastern sovereign-wealth fund in exchange for business. Similarly, in March 2016, Qualcomm settled with the SEC for allegedly giving jobs to relatives of government officials to obtain both government business and government favors in China. Further, HSBC Holdings PLC, JP Morgan, and other financial institutions are facing investigations for supposedly giving jobs to relatives of government officials in exchange for government business or government action.

Wall Street firms disagree with the government's position that their hiring practices are illegal. Banks assert that the government is criminalizing standard hiring practices and that the prosecutions will affect overseas hiring.

Either way, a business can take practical steps to demonstrate that their hiring practices are objective and not a "bribe" intended to obtain government business or government favors, whether the business is working with foreign or domestic governments.

1. Selected Laws and Regulations

Before reviewing these steps, it is important to appreciate the laws and regulations the government may use to mount these prosecutions. Doing so establishes a framework for effective internal controls to manage corruption risk in the hiring process. Although the recent prosecutions have focused on interactions with foreign government officials, similar risks of corruption exist when interacting with federal, state, and local government officials in the United States.

Bribery

Generally, exchanging "anything of value" for government and/or corporate business or government action is bribery, whether the exchange is consummated with a foreign government official or a government official in the United States. The U.S. federal government can use its domestic bribery statute to prosecute instances where an individual or business unlawfully influences a government official to act (or to not act) by offering, promising, or giving something of value. Most states have similar statutes prohibiting bribery.

If a foreign government official is involved, the U.S. government can use the Foreign Corrupt Practices Act, which essentially prohibits offering or promising anything of value to obtain or retain business or to gain a government advantage or to influence a government decision.

Given the settlements with BNY Mellon and Qualcomm, along with the other federal investigations into hiring practices, U.S. prosecutors consider a job or even an internship to be "something of value" that if exchanged for government business or government action merits investigation and possible prosecution.

Ethics Laws

But corruption laws are not the only legal construct that prohibits providing "favors" such as jobs to government officials. Both the U.S. federal government and state and local governments have ethics laws that essentially prohibit government officials from soliciting or accepting, either directly or indirectly, any gratuity, gift, favor, loan, or anything of monetary value from anyone who does business with the government or with any other interests that may be substantially affected by the government official's duties. (See e.g., *Standards of Ethical Conduct* 5 C.F.R. Part 2635; 48 C.F.R. § 3.101; *Conflicts of Interest*, 18 U.S.C. §§ 202-209.) When developing protocols to mitigate the risk of illegal or unethical hiring practices, these ethics laws and regulations should also be considered and incorporated.

3. Definition of Government Official

To adequately address corruption risk around hiring, businesses also need to consider the definition of "government official" and how the business interacts with government officials. Here in the United States, persons elected or appointed to government positions or who work for a government entity are government officials and, for the most part, that is clear.

Identifying who may be a government official when working internationally is not so clear. In many countries the government, a royal family, or a political party may own, manage, or work in business, and they are all considered government officials. Further, the Foreign Corrupt Practices Act defines employees of the U.N., World Bank, and similar organizations as government employees.

Business can interact with government officials as potential customers, customers, or as regulators. However, an often-overlooked relationship with government officials is that a business may actually employ a government official or a close family member of a government official. For example, a business may have a U.S. employee who is the mayor of a small town, a member of a school board, or a member of a port authority commission. All would be considered government officials. Similarly, a business may have an employee with a close family member who is a government official.

4. Internal Controls Requirements

Businesses are not only prohibited from engaging in corrupt activity but are legally mandated to have some system of internal controls that give it assurance that its employees and agents are not acting contrary to the law when interacting with government officials. Further, businesses are expected to have methods to prevent and detect criminal activity and to encourage ethical business conduct and compliance with laws.

Thus, any compliance controls designed to mitigate the risk of improper hiring should include measures to avoid actions that may be construed as a bribe. But the controls also need to include direction on complying with ethics laws and sufficient guidance to identify who may be a government official. Finally, controls should respond to how a business interacts with government officials, to include possibly having employees that are government officials.

5. Steps to Mitigate Improper Hiring

The BNY Mellon and Qualcomm settlement agreements provide insight into the facts the government relied on to prosecute them. A review of these facts will inform businesses of approaches to mitigate key risk areas that may subject a corporation to similar investigations and prosecutions over hiring practices.

BNY Mellon settled, without admitting to SEC claims it violated the FCPA bribery prohibitions and the FCPA internal control requirements because of its hiring practices. According to the settlement, BNY Mellon managed the assets of a Middle Eastern sovereign wealth fund and wanted additional business from the fund. The SEC alleged that the government officials who managed the sovereign wealth funds repeatedly asked BNY Mellon to provide their family members with BNY Mellon internships. The settlement referenced BNY Mellon e-mails that demonstrated BNY Mellon employees believed that by giving the internships to the government officials' family member, BNY Mellon would benefit from additional business from the funds. The SEC also pled in the settlement that BNY Mellon's system of internal controls was so inadequate as to ineffectuate BNY Mellon's anti-bribery policy.

Similarly, Qualcomm settled, without admitting liability, SEC claims that it violated the FCPA bribery prohibitions and the FCPA internal control requirements because of its hiring practices. (The SEC Qualcomm allegations included other allegations beyond hiring practices.) According to the facts in the Qualcomm settlement, government officials from two Chinese state-owned telecommunications enterprises (SOEs), requested that Qualcomm provide internships, educational payments, and eventual full-time employment to their family members. The Qualcomm settlement documents referenced acknowledgment

by Qualcomm employees via e-mails that the internships were important to maintain ongoing business
relationships with the SOEs and certain "customer relationship benefits" would accrue, or be withheld, depending on whether the government official's family
members were hired. The SEC also accused Qualcomm
of not having adequate internal controls to assure its
employees were not providing "anything of value" to
government officials.

It is clear from these settlements that the government now considers a job for a family member of a
government official as "something of value" under
corruption statutes. These cases also reiterate that organizations must have controls in place to avoid running
afoul of corruption laws. Employing these suggestions
on revamping hiring practices may demonstrate to
prosecutors that a business's hiring process is ethical
and legal.

6. Clarify Your Anti-corruption Policy

In its settlement with the government, BNY Mellon
explicitly agreed to address hiring government officials'
relatives in its anti-corruption policy. So, anti-corruption policies should clearly state that hiring someone
in exchange for government business or a government
favor is illegal and violates policy. The policy should
clarify that the business does not give favors, jobs,
money, gifts, entertainment, or anything of value to a
government official, foreign or domestic, in exchange
for some government business or government benefit.

Standardize Aspects of the Hiring Process

The interns that BNY Mellon hired at the behest of the government officials were hired before being interviewed; BNY Mellon sales and client-relationship employees had wide discretion to make initial hiring decisions. Although BNY Mellon had a standard process for hiring interns, apparently these interns did not go through that process. As part of its settlement, BNY Mellon agreed to set up a centralized hiring process so every applicant for a full-time hire or an internship had to be routed through the centralized HR application process.

By creating a standardized application process, a business eliminates the opportunity for employees to independently make hiring decisions for improper reasons. A centralized process that requires recruiting human-resource professionals to manage the hiring process enables hiring recommendations based on objectivity, since human-resource professionals are not involved in the sales process. It also assures that hiring decisions are informed decisions, executed with the subject-matter expertise of those charged with managing human capital for a business (HR) rather than being left to the sales team.

Disclose Relations with Government Officials

BNY Mellon's settlement agreement required that it establish methods for applicants to disclose relationships with government officials and that anti-corruption officers had to review the disclosure, approving any hires with these connections. According to the Qualcomm settlement, one applicant was referred to during the Qualcomm hiring process as "must place" and as having influence with Chinese government officials.

Developing a standard application process that requires applicants to disclose personal or business relationships with government officials and whether the applicant ever worked for the government will furnish recruiting and HR personnel with information to detect hires that may expose the business to charges of corruption. The process should also include steps to conduct further due diligence on the hiring when a relationship with a government official is disclosed. Implementing a two-tiered review system in the hiring process, disclosing relationships and then conducting due diligence on any disclosures, affords the business the opportunity to not only have visibility on hires with relationships with government officials but to have an avenue to review whether the hire is in exchange for government business or government favors.

However, this process must clearly define the relationships that the applicant must disclose because failing to do so will impede the process with too many disclosures. For example, must an applicant disclose a relationship with a cousin, an uncle, or just parents and siblings? This decision should be made on the basis of each business's operations, with regard to questions such as where it does business and how often potential clients refer hires to the business. And the process should be clear on the extent of any due diligence to be conducted on the applicant who discloses a relationship with the government. Finally, the process must define who reviews the due diligence and who has the final word on whether the candidate continues through the hiring process.

Have Written Standards on Who Gets Hired

In both the BNY Mellon case and the Qualcomm case, facts in the settlement documents demonstrate that the hires made at the behest of the government officials did not meet either organization's hiring standards. BNY Mellon required candidates to be from select schools, have a specific GPA, possess leadership skills, and have an affinity for financial services. However, the interns it hired at the request of the government official did not meet these requirements. Likewise, in Qualcomm, the settlement indicated that one candidate hired at the request of the government official had been a "no hire", since the candidate's skills did not match the job.

To avoid the reality or the perception of making a hire in exchange for government business or government favors, an organization should have written, defined education and experience requirements as well as "soft skills" such as leadership ability, emotional intelligence, and maturity. Then, any applicant needs to meet those requirements. Doing so sets a definitive standard for all applicants minimizing the risk of an unqualified person being hired simply because of their connections with a government official.

Conduct Training and Message the Policy and the Processes

The SEC noted in the Qualcomm settlement that certain employees had not been trained on the FCPA. Additionally, Qualcomm did not have a deep enough bench of compliance officers to oversee corruptions risks, so, without this support employees were not well situated to identify potential risks of corruption. BNY Mellon likewise had not trained HR professionals. BNY Mellon was also faulted because it did not assure all employees completed the corruption training and because some employees did not "understand" the training.

Anti-corruption policies and the processes developed to enable compliance with those policies must be systematically communicated throughout the organization and to third parties. The board, executives, employees and third parties need to be given training, messages, and the opportunity to raise questions on corruption policies and adherence to procedures. Employees and leaders in high-risk groups, like recruiting, HR, and business development should be trained more regularly and should receive more regular communications reminding them of the policies and procedures. Further, the training should assure it is effective, that employees understand the requirements and can execute the protocol. This can be done either by conducting live training that includes a question and answer period or through computer-based training that includes testing to complete the course.

Also, it is vital to ensure that all those who must take the training do so, and that the business documents who took the training and who received the communications. In 2012, Morgan Stanley avoided FCPA prosecution because it informed the DOJ of the precise number of times it had tested certain employees on its corruption policies and the precise number of times the offending employees had been reminded about complying with anti-corruption laws.

Monitor Compliance With Policies

According to the Qualcomm settlement, although it had standards around its hiring practices, employees deviated from the standard hiring practices by hiring individuals that did not meet the minimum qualifications of the position.

Having great policies and standard processes will be of no help if employees feel they need not follow them when the right business opportunity presents itself. So, besides creating the policies and procedures designed to help employees avoid corrupt activity, a business needs to conduct regular audits of these policies and procedures to assure employees are not circumventing them. If these audits identify instances of noncompliance, then employees, regardless of their role in the business, need to be disciplined. Further, audit findings should also assess whether the policies and procedures are effective in achieving the goal of hiring without corrupt influence. If the findings reveal that processes are ineffective in doing so, policies and processes should be updated to be responsive.

7. Empower Recruiting and HR to Bring Issues Forward

The SEC alleged in the Qualcomm settlement that Qualcomm HR personnel responded to internal pressure from a vice president to hire a government official's son despite an assessment that the individual would "be a drain on teams." When questioned about the hiring decision, the HR employee explained that "we're operating under a different paradigm here than a normal hire/no hire decision tree." The HR employee was referencing the government official's suggestion that Qualcomm needed to make the hire to continue to benefit from its relationship with the government.

In matters of improper hiring practices, recruiters and HR are the front lines in identifying red flags around a potential hire. Therefore, recruiters and HR professionals must be empowered to question the motives for a particular hire. They also must understand where they can go for legal counsel if they encounter a hiring situation that seems suspicious. Finally, they must be able to seek legal counsel without getting grief for it.

Have Employees Certify to Complying with Policy

BNY Mellon's settlement noted that as part of its annual certification to comply with the BNY Mellon's Code of Conduct, BNY Mellon agreed to have its employees annually certify compliance with the centralized hiring process.

Once a business establishes policies and procedures and trains on those policies and procedures, it should also require employees to annually certify that they have followed the policy and processes. The certification should not only give employees the option to affirm compliance but it should also give employees the option to indicate that before making a certification, they wish to talk with the anti-corruption policy owner's ethics or legal counsel about any actions they are now questioning. Certifications, while valuable, can be harmful if employees are asked to reveal instances of policy violations that may implicate a violation of corruption laws.

8. Document Decisions

In the BNY Mellon settlement, BNY Mellon senior managers had the authority to approve the hires that the government officials had requested without legal, compliance, or HR departments' review of the decision. The SEC claimed that BNY Mellon did not have the controls to assure compliance with law.

A standard hiring process that removes hiring authority from business development and instead requires Human Resources oversight should limit hiring decisions based on illicit requests from government officials. Similarly, having defined hiring criteria, requiring an applicant to disclose relationships with government officials, conducting due diligence on those disclosures, and requiring legal or compliance review of those disclosures creates the controls that assure compliance with the law.

However, to effectively manage these controls and to address instances where it is ethically and legally appropriate to circumvent policy, decisions need to be documented. Further, the standard hiring process should document whether the candidate fit the hiring criteria or not and it should document why the candidate was hired or not hired.

Also, if the decision is made to hire someone without the required background or there was a decision to circumvent hiring processes, the decision and why it was made should be explained and documented. The assessment should include an opinion on the legality of the transaction and the impact a hiring decision, even if legal, would have on the business's reputation.

9. Investigative Processes

Finally, when a recruiting or hiring issue appears to be inconsistent with policy or occurring outside of the standard hiring processes, an organization should have a defined method to investigate the matter. The investigative findings should be documented and any decision, either to hire or to abort the hire, should be noted. Lawyers, consulting with HR and impartial business leaders, need to call foul and stop a hire. Depending on what the investigation reveals and the nature of the business, lawyers will need to work with business leaders to determine if the practices need to be disclosed to the government.

10. Conclusion

Ultimately, an organization needs to analyze its hiring practices, given the U.S. government's increased focus on prosecuting businesses for hiring practices that may violate corruption laws. The review should consider not only the organization's current hiring methods but also the countries where it recruits and hires. But hiring practices in the United States should not be ignored because those, too, can expose a business to a corruption allegation. The review should inform on the need to develop or refine policies and procedures for protecting the business from accusations of illegal or unethical hiring. Compliant and ethical hiring can mitigate the exposure to bribery or other criminal charges or regulatory violations by eliminating trading jobs for government favoritism.

(9) HUMAN RESOURCE MANAGEMENT AND FRAUD

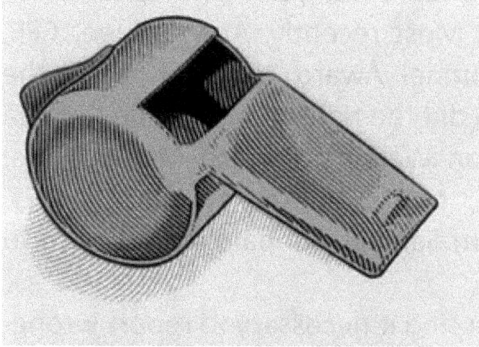

Figure 10. Whistle blowing

One day, you might need to be a whistle-blower. Be forewarned: Your personal and professional lives will suffer. New research on state whistle-blower lawsuits shows it is likely you'll be fired and will lose your case. But then, doing the right thing never meant that right things would happen to you.

Imagine this scenario: A government contractor is overcharging your state government agency for goods and services. You know this because you once worked in the billing department of the contractor. You report this to your supervisor who terminates you shortly afterward. So, you file a complaint with the Florida Commission on Human Relations (FCHR), which reinstates you to your position. Your former employer takes the matter to court under Florida's whistle-blowing law and has you removed again. The court overturns the FCHR's decision because the whistle-blower law requires a complainant to file within 60 days of the alleged incident - and you filed over 100 days later. Also, the FCHR did not have jurisdiction to hear your case. Once again, you are out of a job.

My sample of state-level cases shows that outcomes such as this are not unusual in whistle-blower cases filed in American states. Would-be whistle-blowers might wonder if it's worth it, yet many continue to report wrongdoing. Most recently, Amy Stoupe, CFE, the 2010 ACFE Sentinel Award recipient, blew the whistle. Others who did the right thing include Cynthia Cooper, CFE; Sherron Watkins; Pamela Meyer Davis; Bunny Greenhouse; Marta Andreasen; Dr. David J. Graham; and William Sanjour. All paid a high price to come forward.

As CFEs, we might find it necessary to report wrong-doing, but we should proceed with caution before blowing the whistle. My review of state-level lawsuits suggests that being entitled to protection under a state whistle-blower statute and receiving that protection can be two matters.

1. State whistle-blowing laws

All the U.S. states have laws to protect public employees from retaliation. Most of the state whistle-blowing laws were enacted to encourage public employees to report fraud, waste, and abuse in government agencies. Some laws protect only public employees; others include government contractors and private-sector employees.

Most states also have laws covering private-sector employees. However, many of these laws protect reports involving workplace safety. They were enacted decades ago to protect employees from retaliation when reporting occupational safety issues. Public and private employees can use them, but they might not apply to all situations. Over the years, reporting in other specific situations has been protected.

Many states enacted anti-retaliation clauses for specific claims or industries. For example, Rhode Island has anti-retaliation clauses in statutes pertaining to gaming, nursing homes, health-care facilities, nonprofit hospitals, insurance fraud, health maintenance organizations, and asbestos abatement. Anti-retaliation clauses protect public and private employees working in specific cases.

2. The essence of blowing that whistle

Whistleblowing, as it relates to fraud, is the act of reporting fraud, waste, and abuse. Reporting any act of wrongdoing is considered whistleblowing, regardless if it is reported by a public or private employee or to persons inside or outside of the victim organization.

Anyone can report wrongdoing, but the level of protection an employee will receive will differ depending on whether they're public or private, to whom they report, the manner in which they report, the wrongdoing they report, and the law under which they report.

Take the Texas Whistle-blower Act, for example. It protects public employees from retaliation who report violations of law to appropriate law enforcement agencies, providing the employee files a grievance within 90 days of when the employer's adverse employment action occurred or was discovered by the employee. The employee must sue under the grievance or appeal process of the governmental employer before suing.

The employee must also report the violation in good faith, prove the retaliation results from the whistleblowing, and identify the laws violated and the persons engaged in the violations. Employees can be compensated for their losses, but the entity can defend itself by asserting its actions were unrelated to the whistleblowing. This is an affirmative defense that can be asserted by any employer. Employers using an affirmative defense will admit they took the adverse personnel action but claim the action was due to events independent of the whistleblowing. If you find Texas' Whistle-blowing Law daunting, you're probably not alone. My review of state-level lawsuits filed by whistle-blowers shows that it's difficult to receive protection under many of the state laws.

3. Most whistle-blowers are fired

Seventy-four percent of the whistle-blowers in my review were terminated. Another 6 percent were suspended, and five percent were transferred against their wishes. The remaining 15 percent were given poor evaluations, demoted, or harassed. The results, summarized in **Exhibit 1 (below)**, indicate that retaliation occurs, although this review cannot determine how often.

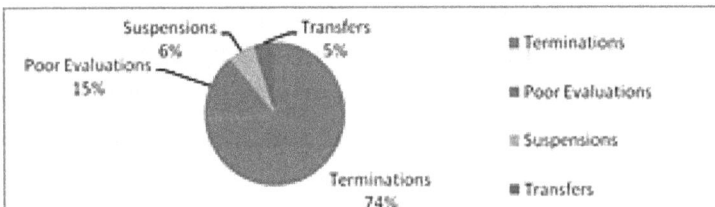

Approximately 60 percent of the lawsuits were filed in the past ten years; however, it is impossible to say why employees are increasingly turning to the courts to solve their problems. Perhaps employees are reporting wrongful acts more frequently and filing more frivolous lawsuits. It is also possible that employers are committing more acts of wrongdoing and retaliating more often. Then again, it is possible the rise is due to the increasingly litigious nature of American society.

The whistle-blowers in this sample did not fare well in their lawsuits. Fifty-five percent lost their cases. Fourteen percent lost because they failed to prove their cases. Eleven percent failed to prove a causal connection between the alleged retaliation and the whistleblowing. Only 22 percent won their lawsuits. Of these, two percent were reinstated to their old jobs and 8 percent won damage awards. The remaining 23 percent were remanded for a new trial.

To prevail, employees will probably have to link their whistleblowing to the retaliation. This can be difficult for employees having problems in the workplace because employers will claim their adverse personnel actions were based on the employees' poor performances, not the employees' decisions to blow the whistle. It is especially easy for employers to assert this claim if the person who conducted the retaliation claims no knowledge of the whistleblowing.

4. Get technicalities correct

Twenty-two percent of the whistle-blowers lost because they didn't comply with some technicality in the laws.

The laws are extremely specific on how whistle-blowers must report the wrongdoing. Violating any aspect of the law will cause a loss of protection.

Six percent of the employees lost because they failed to exhaust all their internal remedies before reporting their concerns externally. Many laws require the employee to report internally first to allow the employer to correct the matter. This minimizes the potentially devastating impact that public reports can have on organizations when the claims do not have merit or could be handled more effectively internally. Internal reports can also allow the employer to conceal the unlawful activity, if they are so inclined.

Another five percent lost because they failed to report the act of wrongdoing correctly. Some laws require the witness to report the wrongdoing in writing within a certain period of time after it's discovered. Other laws require the whistle-blower to state the specific laws broken. These requirements provide the employer with specificity so they can correct the problem.

Case in point: A high-level officer, working for a government defense contractor, discovered that his employer was overbilling the government, supplying defective parts, and engaging in the unauthorized use of government equipment. He refused to participate in the activities and reported them to his employer's government liaison officer only to find himself terminated afterward. He sued under Florida's whistle-blower law and lost because he failed to first inform his employer of the alleged activity in writing.

Five percent of the employees in the sample lost because they filed their lawsuits using inappropriate laws. Choosing an appropriate law sounds easy, but that isn't always the case.

Case in point: A flight engineer, working for a Florida-based airline (and living in the state), was terminated after he insisted on delaying a flight at New York's John F. Kennedy Airport to repair the plane's hydraulic system. He filed his suit in a Florida court under a New York State labor law because Florida did not have a whistle-blower law. The court dismissed his complaint, and the engineer appealed. Meanwhile, Florida enacted a whistle-blower law covering private-sector employees. The case went all the way to the Florida Supreme Court, but the engineer lost because Florida's whistle-blower law did not apply retroactively.

5. Private–sector employees have it tough

Most whistle-blower laws should protect public-sector employees who report violations affecting public health and safety. Proving public interest is easy for public-sector employees because their work involves public protection. It's not as easy for private-sector employees. Eleven percent of the private-sector whistle-blowers in the sample lost their cases because the matters didn't involve public policy. The case of two nurses working in a private nursing home exemplifies the difficulties private-sector employees can have winning in court, even when their cases appear to involve public interest.

Case in point: A hospital fired one of its therapists six days after he told representatives from an accrediting organization (during a site visit) that the hospital's therapists completed patient charts during their shifts rather than immediately after treating patients as required by the accrediting organization.

The therapist, who had worked for the hospital for 23 years, sued for retaliation and lost because he could not convince the courts that charting was a matter of public policy. The therapist argued that the Illinois Medical Patient's Rights Act gives patients the right to sound and consistent care and failing to immediately chart jeopardizes patient care. The court said it wasn't enough to claim a broad or generalized public policy.

To prevail, the therapist needed to show how a lack of immediate charting violates an Illinois state law, and the therapist was not able to find an Illinois law that requires immediate charting. Only the courts can decide whether an issue is a matter of public policy, and this court was not willing to find it so.

Five percent of the private-sector employees in this sample lost because they mistakenly filed charges under statutes that covered only public employees. Not all the laws protect private-sector employees. Whistle-blowers need to make sure they are covered by the laws they use.

6. Whistle-blowers try to protect public interest

Eighty-five percent involved issues of public health, safety, or interest. Twenty-five percent involved public safety. Fifteen percent involved public health. Sixteen percent involved the misappropriation of public funds. Eighteen percent involved matters of general public interest, and eleven percent involved civil rights violations.

Public employees filed 60 percent of the cases in the sample, and they witnessed the most serious violations of public policy. Public engineers reported the most serious offenses. These incidents usually involved public exposure to toxic chemicals or waste. Public nurses also reported serious issues. Their complaints usually involved patient neglect and fatal accidents. The complaints of police officers were also very serious and usually involved internal corruption.

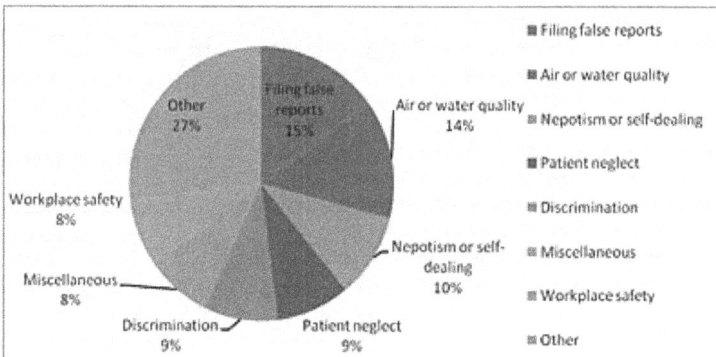

Figure 11. Violation of public policy

Damage awards were often given to whistle-blowers who reported serious public policy issues. An analyst in a California public housing authority, for example, reported that someone was leaking confidential bid information. The whistle-blower was fired but was awarded a $1.3 million damage award in court. In Pennsylvania, a housing authority employee reported self-dealing and received a $900,000 damage award for being terminated. These awards were given to whistle-blowers reporting irregularities involving public funds.

Large awards were also given to whistle-blowers reporting violations of public health and safety. A Connecticut water treatment plant engineer was terminated after reporting plant managers for concealing that the town's water supply was inadequately treated. The court awarded the engineer $127,000 for lost wages. These awards support the assertion that whistle-blowers are public employees attempting to resolve serious violations of public policy.

The violations summarized in **Exhibit 2 (above)** show that 15 percent of the employees accused their employers of issuing false reports. Fourteen percent alleged violations involving air or water quality. Ten percent alleged nepotism or self-dealing. Nine percent alleged patient abuse or neglect. Nine percent alleged discrimination or civil rights violations. Eight percent alleged miscellaneous violations and another eight percent alleged violation of state labor laws or workplace safety.

7. The laws used by whistle-blowers

Examining the laws whistle-blowers use to seek protection can provide insights into why they often lost their cases. Sixty-one percent of the whistle-blowers sued using a state whistle-blower law. Twelve percent used an anti-retaliation clause in a labor law. Eight percent sued under contract law, and 5 percent sued under the U.S. Constitution or other civil rights law. Five percent began by having their cases heard in a civil service or union hearing, and 2 percent sued to appeal a professional code of conduct violation. The remaining 7 percent filed under a miscellaneous law. The laws are summarized in **Exhibit 3 (below.)**

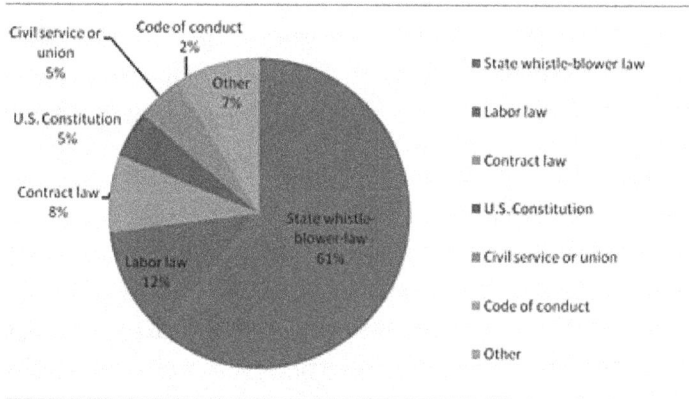

Sixty-four percent of the whistle-blowers who sued using a labor or employment law lost, although they barely blew the whistle. In most of these cases, the employees were terminated shortly after beginning their inquiries, but they didn't lose for making unsubstantiated allegations. They lost because the matters in their cases weren't of public interest.

Case in point: An auditor, working for a New York City brokerage firm, reported that corporate officers were engaged in money laundering. The firm terminated him, even though the firm's policy manual specifically prohibited retaliation against employees investigated. He filed a complaint with the New York Stock Exchange and received compensatory damages in arbitration. He then sued under a labor law to seek punitive damages. The auditor lost because punitive damages are awarded only when the perpetrator engages in a pattern of conduct aimed at the public in general. The whistle-blower was not able to prove sufficient public interest.

The whistle-blowers in the sample who sued under contract law were independent contractors. They sued for breach of contract when they were terminated before the end of their employment contracts and lost when they failed to prove the causal link between their termination and whistleblowing. Some courts allowed the employers to terminate these employees "at will" despite their employment contracts.

Case in point: The most interesting contract law case was filed by mechanics of a chemical company. They told the Occupational Safety and Health Administration (OSHA) that their employer exposed the chemical plant shop to asbestos, and then they were terminated. The employees could have filed a claim under OSHA, the Texas whistle-blowing law, or contract law. They sued for breach of contract because under contract law they only had to prove: 1) that they had an employment agreement 2) the employer interfered with that agreement and 3) the employer's interference resulted in damages. The mechanics proved their case and were awarded compensatory damages for lost wages. It wasn't clear from the case, but it's likely they also were reinstated to their positions.

Some of the whistle-blowers sued to protect their rights to free speech under the First Amendment of the U.S. Constitution. These employees claimed the employer's retaliation violated their right to free speech. To prevail, these whistle-blowers had to prove the issue was a matter of public interest. That was not always easy.

Case in point: A Utah firefighter, for example, claimed that his department's new protocol for handling wildfires was unsafe. The court looked to whether the employer's interest in promoting efficiency outweighed the employee's right to voice public concerns and decided that the way the firefighter voiced his concerns undermined efficiency and morale. The firefighter had secretly tape-recorded conversations with co-workers and jumped the chain of command. The court held that the firefighter had carried his concerns to protect the public too far.

In another First Amendment case, a Nebraska prison guard told a reporter about the serious racial problems in his prison. The guard was terminated, although he had permission to participate in the interview. Prison officials claimed the guard overstepped his authority to speak in the interview and that his speech disrupted prison efficiency. The court held that racial problems are a matter of public interest and outweigh any harmful effects to prison efficiency or morale. The guard was reinstated and awarded attorney's fees.

Most of the whistle-blowers who began their complaints with civil service or union hearings were police officers, alleging harassment after reporting internal corruption. The officers lost at hearing and sued to appeal those decisions. Most officers were assigned to task forces charged with investigating internal corruption. They were harassed when the investigations led to findings of internal corruption. All but one lost on appeal because a higher court won't overturn a lower court's decision unless it's arbitrary. The only officer to prevail demonstrated a long pattern of harassment, which led to his complete mental and physical breakdown. Although the officers usually lost pursuing this course of action, as civil servants they likely had to begin with civil service or union grievances.

OUTCOME OF THE LAWSUITS						
The Laws used to File	Won	Reinstate	Damages	Remand	Lost	Total
State Whistle-blower Law	7%	2%	8%	28%	55%	100%
Labor Law	0%	0%	9%	27%	64%	100%
Contract Law	12%	25%	13%	13%	37%	100%
U.S. Constitution	40%	0%	0%	0%	60%	100%
Civil Service or Union	40%	0%	0%	0%	60%	100%
Code of Conduct	50%	0%	0%	0%	50%	100%
Other	0%	0%	0%	50%	50%	100%

Table 2. Tracking lawsuits results

Most employees who sued to appeal decisions that their whistleblowing violated professional codes of conduct lost when the codes required the professionals to maintain client confidentiality. The whistle-blowers argued that employers aren't clients, and the codes don't require employee-employer confidentiality. The courts still held these employees to a higher standard of confidentiality. So far, the courts have applied this standard to attorneys, but other professionals with confidentiality clauses in their codes of conduct, such as accountants, could be held to this standard.

Most of the whistle-blowers in the review lost their lawsuits. **Exhibit 4 (above)** shows that 55 percent of the whistle-blowers filing under a state whistle-blower statute lost their cases. Sixty-four percent filing under a labor law lost, as did 60 percent of those filing under the U.S. Constitution or civil service agreement. Half of the employees appealing a violation of a professional code of conduct lost.

This review could not determine why the whistle-blowers used the wrong laws or filed in inappropriate courts. Many of the whistle-blowers could have been more successful had they been smarter about what and where to file. Several factors play a role in deciding under what law and in which court to file. These are issues of jurisdiction and venue and are discussed in "Deciding Where to File" below.

8. Research the details

Whistle-blowers can improve their chances of success by preparing early and reading the whistle-blowing laws. The case law is also important because it shows the precedent already set by the courts. The better prepared you are, the less likely you'll make avoidable mistakes.

Case in point: One whistle-blower made a fatal mistake when he filed charges against the individuals who committed the wrongdoing rather than his employer. Had he researched the law, he would have known that the term "employers," as used in Massachusetts' law that reads "an employer shall not take retaliatory action against an employee..." means the commonwealth and its agencies or political subdivision. Therefore, under the law, the allegations had to be lodged against the employer, rather than the individual offenders. Unfortunately, he filed against the offending employees and lost his case.

Another whistle-blower lost because he filed claims in two venues only to learn later that seeking protection under one statute precluded protection under another statute. This whistle-blower filed a claim alleging retaliatory discharge under the Minnesota Whistle-blower Act and a claim of reprisal discrimination under the Minnesota Human Rights Act (MHRA.) The whistle-blower presented the claims in court and received favorable decisions on both claims. The employer appealed and the Supreme Court decided that the exclusivity clause in the MHRA barred filing any other claims on the matter.

An Ohio guidance counselor lost because she failed to prove that she suffered damages from the retaliation. The Ohio law states that a claim of retaliation can be brought only where the employee suffers a direct monetary loss. The Ohio whistle-blower did not suffer a financial loss because every time the school district assigned her to a distant work location, she complained and was reassigned closer to home.

An evolving issue is the extent to which whistle-blowers must be certain of violations. Many laws already require the employee to state the specific law broken. Some courts require whistle-blowers to be certain of their allegations. Trends requiring certainty will make it increasingly difficult for whistle-blowers to receive protection. (See "Know the Facts before you Blow the Whistle" below.)

9. Don't get caught with unclean hands!

Five percent of the whistle-blowers failed to receive protection because of their improper conduct. Some of these whistle-blowers misused their employers' property; some stole it. Employees must ensure their conduct is above scrutiny because some courts will apply the "doctrine of unclean hands" and bar whistle-blowers from protection if they've engaged in misconduct directly related to their complaints.

Case in point: A California quality assurance manager secretly copied confidential patient records to prove that a near-fatal incident was caused by human error after her hospital-employer appeared to dodge an investigation. The manager pursued an investigation and was fired a few weeks later. The manager sued for wrongful termination and barely prevailed. The lower court applied the doctrine of unclean hands and ruled for the hospital. The manager appealed. The appeals court didn't dismiss the case but limited what the employee could recover because of her unclean hands.

The doctrine of unclean hands can work against employers, just as it does employees. In 2001, a Florida health-care agency submitted documents containing incorrect information to the court. The whistle-blower proved the information was false and won her case on those grounds alone. Thus, it is important for employers and employees to comport themselves with integrity.

Whistle-blowers who commit unlawful acts to advance their cases do not do well in court, but neither do whistle-blowers who refuse to commit unlawful acts on behalf of their employers. Most state whistle-blower laws protect employees that refuse to commit unlawful acts, but it is difficult to receive that protection.

Case in point: A Texas deckhand was asked to pump the bilges of the boat into the water, despite a placard on the boat, which stated that pumping bilges into the water was illegal. The deckhand confirmed with the U.S. Coast Guard that the practice was illegal. The deckhand refused to pump the bilges and was fired. He sued for wrongful discharge and prevailed because the court upheld the public policy doctrine that prevents the termination of at-will employees for refusing to perform illegal acts.

The deckhand above prevailed, but many others haven't been as fortunate. A Florida tugboat captain, for example, was fired after he refused to make an 18-hour trip in contravention to the federal safety regulations. The captain lost in court, even though the Florida whistle-blower law states that employers can't retaliate against employees for refusing to participate in unlawful activities. Employees such as the tugboat captain might avoid breaking the law, but they may have to sacrifice their jobs to do so.

10. Implications

The review of this sample of cases helps provide important insights into actual whistle-blowing incidents. The review shows that even when well-intentioned employees feel they are doing the right thing by reporting acts of wrongdoing, their reports aren't always well received. The findings also suggest that employees who witness acts of wrongdoing should seek legal counsel before acting.

The cases involved no whistle-blowers who also was CFEs, but CFEs might run into the same problems. CFEs should learn when, where, and how to report fraudulent acts before they blow the whistle, so they can comply with the procedures required to receive protection.

This review looked at only a sample of the state-level cases filed against employers for retaliation. But it does highlight that whistle-blower cases can be difficult to prove, and that all involved (including CFEs) should be knowledgeable about the laws involved and seek legal guidance early.

- **Subject Matter Jurisdiction** – Courts must have power to hear the issue in your suit. Subject matter jurisdiction is based on the law you plan to use. Generally, federal courts hear violations of federal laws and state courts hear violations of state laws, although this isn't always the case. Employees can file alleged violations of their civil rights in state or federal courts under Section 1983 of Title 42 of the U.S. Code of Federal Regulations. While rarely used today, Section 1983 is part of the Civil Rights Act and the primary means of enforcing all Constitutional rights. Subject Matter Jurisdiction can help employees file in federal or state court. The employer might ask to have the case moved to another court.

- **Personal Jurisdiction** – Make sure the court has power over the party you want to sue. A court must have personal jurisdiction over the defendant to hear a case. Courts usually have personal jurisdiction over the people and organizations residing or doing business in their jurisdiction.
- **Venue** – Venue refers to the court that will hear your case. The proper venue is the jurisdiction in which the defendant lives or does business, the contract was signed or carried out, or the incident took place. More than one court can have jurisdiction over your case. Pick the venue most convenient for you.

11. Know the Facts before You Blow the Whistle

An Ohio prosecutor gathered payroll records he believed proved his co-workers were overstating their wages. The attorney reported the allegations to the local police department and was fired. When the case went to trial, the attorney was denied whistle-blower protection because he failed to investigate his suspicions. The court said if he had made reasonable internal inquiries before reporting his suspicions externally, he would have learned that his co-workers were not committing payroll fraud and he wouldn't have reported externally. The prosecutor was denied protection under Ohio's whistle-blower law because the law specifically states that employees must make good faith efforts to determine the accuracy of the information they are reporting, and a failure to make such an effort could lead to disciplinary action, including termination.

12. Doing the Right Thing Can Get You Fired

A scientist in charge of environmental health for a large U.S. oil refinery in New Jersey learned his employer was supplying Japan with gasoline containing dangerously high levels of benzene, a carcinogen in gasoline. He told some Japanese managers about this at an industry conference in Japan. The Japanese managers said they couldn't reduce the benzene because it was too expensive.

The scientist knew that Japan didn't require warning labels, vapor containment systems, or catalytic converters. He also knew that New Jersey's state laws and international treaties prohibited marketing gasoline with unsafe levels of benzene. The scientist advised the Japanese managers to stop using the gasoline until it could reduce the benzene.

When the scientist returned from Japan, he was immediately restricted from his employer's premises and given an "indefinite special assignment." Two weeks later, he was terminated. The scientist sued under New Jersey's Conscientious Employee Protection Act and was awarded $2.5 million in compensatory damages, $875,000 for emotional distress, and $3.5 million in punitive damages, despite his employer's alleged unawareness of the scientist's comments at the conference.

(10) GOOD GOVERNANCE FOR CORPORATE GROWTH

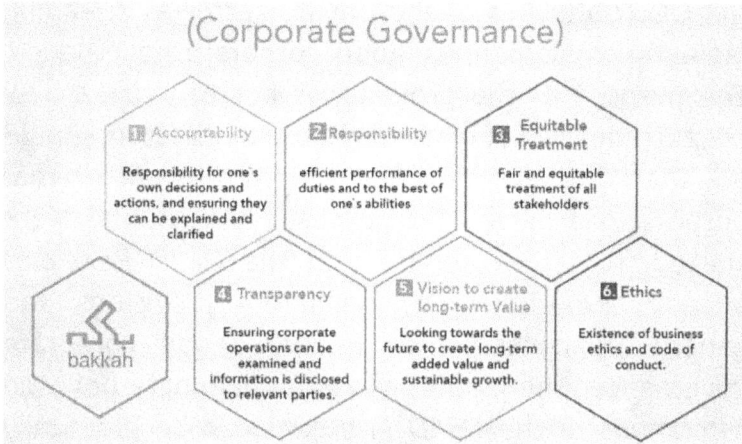

Figure 12. Factors mitigating for

During the last decade, the OECD has taken the lead among international organizations to promote good corporate governance. The OECD Principles of Corporate Governance *has become the global bench-mark, accepted in OECD and non-OECD countries. These accomplishments result from a close partnership with the business community and other stakeholders. We have, therefore, called on a group of business leaders to give their perspective on how to apply the OECD Principles in the boardroom. Corporate boards will face a diversity of situations and challenges. We wanted to learn about real stories that can provide guidance and advice to those vested with the responsibility of running an efficient board in a corporate organization.*

Introduction

In October 2004, OECD member countries invited a business-sector group on boardroom practices to promote the use of the *OECD Principles* among board members. The initiative reflects the importance that the OECD attaches to the private sector as a leading factor in implementing good corporate governance. The purpose of the project was not to write a new code or checklist of what the board of directors should do. There are already a multitude of documents that purport to achieve that purpose. Instead, the work started from the premise that the *OECD Principles* already comprise those regulatory provisions and generic principles which underlie good corporate governance. The intention was to illuminate how the aspirations of the *OECD Principles* can be practically achieved in different regulatory, economic, and cultural contexts, within which directors face similar challenges. The experiences of directors and practitioners in using the *OECD Principles* in a world necessarily characterized by incomplete law are of particular importance. How do board members, in performing their everyday functions, fill the gaps that laws, regulations and guidelines cannot, and should not, fill? It is hoped that the experiences provided in this volume will be useful guidance regarding how directors can discharge their responsibilities.

1. Strategic guidance

OECD Principle VI: The corporate governance framework should ensure the strategic guidance of the

company, the effective monitoring of management by the board, and the board's accountability to the company and the shareholders.

> ➤ *Board structures and procedures vary both within and among OECD countries. Some countries have two-tier boards that separate the super-visory function and the management functions into different bodies. Such systems typically have a "supervisory board" composed of nonexecu-tive board members and a "management board" composed of executives. Other countries have "unitary" boards, which bring together execu-tive and non-executive board members. In some countries there is also an additional statutory body for audit. The* OECD Principles *are suffi-ciently general to apply to whatever board struc-ture is charged with the functions of governing the enterprise and monitoring management.*

Choosing between a unitary board and a two-tier board

"Some countries allow a choice between a unitary board and a two-tier board structure. In making this decision, the board should consider what is best for that partic-ular company. For example, a unitary board may be more suitable if investors of the company understand the unitary board system better. Whichever system is adopted, the board should ensure that it explains the structure to investors so that they can understand and appreciate how the system works and how the board sees its role." (Dr. Roland Koestler)

Combining a unitary board with a two-tier board

"Some companies have major operations in countries requiring a unitary board as well as in countries that mandate a two-tier board; in such cases, it may be possible to structure the company in a way that incorporates features of both systems. For example, a company may have two holding companies (one in each country) and two boards of directors that operate as one and are comprised of people who are directors of both holding companies. The two holding companies may enter into agreements to equalize the rights of shareholders of both companies with respect to dividends, voting, and liquidation, and may also guarantee each other's borrowings. In addition, shareholder resolutions, such as director elections, passed at one holding company may be made conditional on approval at the other holding company. A separate proxy statement is issued for each annual meeting, while it may be possible to produce a combined annual report, provided both sets of regulators agree that the contents satisfy all applicable regulatory requirements. Other companies may instead interpose a holding company with one board of directors beneath the two ultimate holding companies, with shareholders owning shares in the holding company." (Alison Dillon)

In guiding corporate strategy, the board is chiefly responsible for monitoring managerial performance and achieving an adequate return for shareholders, while preventing conflicts of interest and balancing competing demands on the corporation. For boards to effectively fulfil their responsibilities they must be able to exercise objective and independent judgement.

Another important board responsibility is to oversee systems designed to ensure that the corporation obeys laws, including tax, competition, labor, environmental, equal opportunity, health and safety laws. In some countries, companies have found it useful to explicitly articulate the responsibilities that the board assumes and those for which management is accountable.

Board mandate:

"The board should develop a list of board responsibilities so there is clarity as to what is the responsibility of the board and what the responsibility of management is. Developing such a list is a useful way of ensuring that everyone understands their role and is not stepping on anyone's toes, and that there are no surprises." (Jack Krol)

"The board should be responsible for those tasks that are unique to the board. These tasks should be clearly stated as being the responsibility of the board. Such tasks may include selecting and evaluating the CEO, ensuring that the company's strategy is relevant and appropriate, monitoring strategic risk management by the CEO and ensuring that any limitations on delegation to the CEO are in place and functioning. For example, the board may establish an ethics committee to ensure that particular internal controls limiting executive behavior are effective.

At some companies, the board is required to make operational decisions such as capital expenditures, where the amount involved crosses a certain materiality threshold. At other companies, the board does not get involved in any capital expenditure decisions, no matter how large the amount, unless specifically requested by the CEO – in such cases, the board assumes that management has conducted the financial analysis correctly and board consideration of the issue would add no value. Such boards may instead require decisions with non-financial implications to be brought to its attention, such as issues relating to employment, health and safety, the environment and/or the company's reputation." (Anonymous Contributor)

"The board mandate should be clear and in writing. For example, it may stipulate that the board is one group sharing common objectives that reviews how the business is run –but does not run the business itself – by:

- *Agreeing on the strategic framework and keeping it under vigorous review*
- *Monitoring the implementation of strategy through the operational plans*
- *Focusing on long-term sustainable value creation*
- *Safeguarding the longer-term values of the company, which include the brand and corporate reputation*
- *Overseeing the quality of management and how it is maintained at world class levels*
- *Maintaining a governance framework that facilitates substance and not merely form; and*
- *The overriding theme of the board should be profitable growth within an acceptable risk profile." - Niall FitzGerald*

"The board's role can be visualized in three dimensions: first, a contributing dimension, where directors bring to bear their expertise and experience to enhance the company's wealth-creating capabilities; second, a counselling dimension, where directors counsel on the approaches the CEO plans to adopt with respect to specific initiatives, so that the wealth-creating processes are smooth and within the company's values; and third, the controlling dimension, where the board exercises its surveillance functions to ensure created wealth passes through to the rightful claimants without undue leakage." - Dr. N. Balasubramanian

Board mandate in controlled companies:
"In a controlled company, the board should discuss the list of board responsibilities with the dominant owner and negotiate with the owner where required to obtain his or her agreement." (Jack Krol)

"The board of a family-controlled company that is in transition to becoming a public company should beware the temptation to continue former management habits such as discussing issues at a level that is overly detailed for a company with separate ownership and control. Board involvement with issues that are properly within the province of management results in inefficient board processes and requires devotion of an excessive amount of meeting time. Instead, the board should structure its agenda at the outset to ensure that it focuses on issues such as strategic planning and risk management." (José Monforte)

An example of the line between oversight and management – consumer advertising:

"Directors are often fascinated by consumer advertising – it is a subject on which everyone is an expert! It would, however, be fatal to allow directors any say whatsoever in the execution of advertising. That is a management function. There is, however, a policy aspect to advertising which is a proper matter for the board to discuss and on which to rule, because advertising is part of the public face of a company and has consequences for the way in which the company is perceived by the community.

Therefore, the board needs to be aware of the advertising going out in the name of the company and is entitled to take a view as to whether that advertising is in keeping with the standards of the company. Advertising policy is a matter for the board, while advertising execution is the responsibility of management. The line between policy and execution is not always easy to draw in practice but it is the duty of the chair to protect management from board interference in matters delegated to management." (Adrian Cadbury)

"Consumer advertising policy can sometimes be the responsibility of the board, because of its potential impact on the reputation of the company. Advertising products overseas may require extra attention, as what is acceptable in one country may be viewed as offensive in another." (Ira M. Millstein)

The board is not only accountable to the company and its shareholders but also must act in their best interests. In addition, boards are expected to take due regard of, and deal fairly with, other stakeholder interests including those of employees, creditors, customers, suppliers, and local communities. Observance of environmental and social standards is relevant in this context.

Social responsibility:
"Companies should be aware that what seems to be a straightforward approach to a social responsibility issue may have unintended consequences. For example, one company may tackle the issue of child labor by switching from a supplier that uses child labor to a supplier that does not; however, such a switch can leave destitute those children who no longer have work. In contrast, another company may choose to employ children and provide them with regulated wages, schooling, and reasonable working hours and conditions." (Adrian Cadbury)

"At some companies, social responsibility is integrated into the company's business and is included in management's list of strategic goals. At other companies, social responsibility may roll alongside – but not feed into – the business, and it may be the responsibility of a designated manager. Either way, companies should strive to make social responsibility part of the corporate culture from the very beginning. It is more difficult for companies to create a culture of responsibility down the track." (Alison Dillon)

Social responsibility and relations with shareholders:
"Social responsibility issues, in particular, fair competition and the environment, are important to each company's long-range value and should be discussed

on a regular basis with shareholders. There should be greater focus on avoiding future problems, and less looking backwards to find problems that occurred in the past. In addition, shareholders should understand that they have a key role to play in supporting social responsibility initiatives, which should in turn positively impact the value of their portfolios in the long term." (Sir Mark Moody-Stuart)

Social responsibility and philanthropy:
"Social responsibility and philanthropy are two different things, although both can result in reputational benefits to a company as well as social benefits to the community. For example, social responsibility encompasses corporate efforts to reduce emissions or energy intake in the operation of the company, while philanthropy relates to humanitarian, educational, scientific, or other causes supported by the company." (Laura Cha)

"The board should ensure that it consults with shareholders and employees of the company as well as relevant stakeholders with respect to philanthropic initiatives. Corporate philanthropy should, as far as practicable, be somewhat related to the company's present and future business interests. If not, it may be preferable to allow individual shareholders and stakeholders to choose their own beneficiaries according to their personal beliefs and convictions." (Dr. N. Balasubramanian)

Operating in developing countries and mature markets:

"Before attempting to do business in a developing country, the company should determine whether it is permitted to do the scope of business it wants to do in that country, as some developing countries impose narrow limits on corporate activity. For example, a company in a developing country may be permitted to build a plant in only one place to ensure job creation in that region or make only one particular product.

If a company is directed by a government body to do something it does not like, it should avoid doing it. For example, if a company is only permitted to build a factory in a region where there is corruption, destruction of property, and/or violence against the company's employees, the company should consider whether to cancel its plan to build that factory or build it in another country." (Jack Krol)

"A company should not assume that it can afford to relax compliance and monitoring standards when operating in a sophisticated market. A company that focuses heavily on safety and compliance with respect to its operations in developing countries (such as using monitors) should also ensure that it pays attention to its operations in mature markets. For example, a company that does not take seriously safety and financial controls in developed markets, on the assumption that a developed market has adequate regulations, may discover the hard way that the market does not –such a company may find itself facing myriad operational and reputational issues when problems arise such as allegations of bribery or an exploding factory." (Anonymous Contributor)

Operating in countries with weak government 1:
"A company that wishes to operate successfully over the long-term in a country with weak government should ensure that there is a perceived benefit from the presence of the company in that country. The company's operations should benefit the central government (through taxation) and local communities (through employment, training and the supply chain.)

Facilitating operations from which these benefits flow may be helpful to a government seeking re-election, which may in turn assist companies to win government contracts at the expense of competitors offering corrupt upfront payments to government officials but whose operations may not be as beneficial to the electorate. Companies should understand that operating in a country that is essentially corrupt is not always an unwinnable battle, because not every person in a corrupt country will be corrupt and companies may attract support by refusing to engage in corrupt behavior.

Companies should also strive to mitigate, eliminate, or compensate for any negative impacts that may flow from operations. For example, a company operating in a country where conditions necessitate the presence of armed forces on company premises should take steps to reduce the risk of security abuses by providing training that emphasizes human rights and safety.

Companies operating in countries with weak governments sometimes face widespread corruption, human rights abuses, security problems, and other issues. A practical method of counteracting a specific issue may be to form a coalition with other companies, shareholders, non-governmental organizations and governments –including the government of the host country, where possible– to exchange experiences and develop potential long-term solutions to the issue. Coalitions should start with solutions that are voluntary and work towards gradually building sound legislation that will be effectively implemented and enforced. Governments are usually more likely to view coalition efforts at reform more favorably than those of an individual corporation, which may be viewed as seeking reform to further its own particular interests.

For example, various coalitions around the world have developed voluntary principles relating to corruption, human rights, labor conditions, security, and the environment, and encourage disclosure by companies with respect to adherence to the principles (for example, in sustainability reports that are distributed to shareholders.) Some coalitions also assess the extent to which companies and/or countries comply with voluntary principles and publish these assessments." (Sir Mark Moody-Stuart)

The "baseline" of compliance:

"Compliance with laws and regulations will not guarantee success but should be the baseline for companies to adhere to. Some companies think they are being clever by superficially complying with laws and regulations, but this can lead to complications, particularly where things go wrong." (Anonymous Contributor)

Political donations:
"Companies may make political donations where appropriate, provided donations are disclosed and/or approved by shareholders as required. For example, a company operating in a fledgling democracy with little resources may wish to support the democratic process by providing political donations to both the government and opposition parties in equal amounts. Political donations should be treated with caution, as they may give rise to expectations that a company will continue to make donations in the future." (Sir Mark Moody-Stuart)

2– Acting in the interest of the company and shareholders

OECD Principle VI.A: Directors should act on an informed basis, in good faith, with due diligence and care, and in the best interest of the company and the shareholders.

In some countries, the board is legally required to act in the interest of the company, considering the interests of shareholders, employees, and the public good. Acting in the best interest of the company should not permit management to become entrenched. This principle states the two key elements of the fiduciary duty of board members: the duty of care and the duty of loyalty.

The duty of care requires board members to act on an informed basis, in good faith, with due diligence and care. In some jurisdictions there is a standard of reference which is the behavior that a reasonably prudent person would exercise in similar circumstances. In nearly all jurisdictions, the duty of care does not extend to errors of business judgement if board members are not grossly negligent and a decision is made with due diligence, etc. The principle calls for board members to act on an informed basis. Good practice thinks that they should be satisfied that key corporate information and compliance systems are sound and underpin the key monitoring role of the board advocated by the OECD Principles. In many jurisdictions this meaning is already considered an element of the duty of care, while in others it is required by securities regulation, accounting standards, etc.

> *The duty of loyalty is of central importance, since it underpins effective implementation of other principles in this document relating to, for example, the equitable treatment of shareholders, monitoring of related party transactions, and the establishment of remuneration policy for key executives and board members. It is also a key principle for board members working within the structure of a group of companies: even though a company might be controlled by another enterprise, the duty of loyalty for a board member relates to the company and all its shareholders and not to the controlling company of the group.*

The risk of "analysis paralysis"

"Requiring directors to be 'fully-informed' may be misleading, because it is not possible for directors to undertake all of the analysis that may be possible –this may lead to 'analysis paralysis.' It is the role of management to fully analyze information, while the role of the director is to ask questions and seek second and third opinions where required before making a decision. For example, the directors of a company with a cheered history asked so many questions of management on every decision that was brought to the board that the number of agenda items quadrupled, and the board became dysfunctional." (Charnchai Charuvastr)

Duty of care in the sale of a company:

"If the board has made a judgement that the sale of the company is in the best interests of all of the shareholders, the board should first obtain a view independent of management as to the value of the company and should utilize a sale method or process designed to generate the most value for shareholders. Management's view as to the value of the company will be relevant and management will work closely with outside advisors to execute the sale process." (Peter Dey)

3. The duty of loyalty and competition

"Directors owe an undivided loyalty to the company that requires that they consider only what is in the best interests of the company in making decisions. Problems related to a director's loyalty usually arise from a director's particular interest in a decision before the board, for example as a party to a particular transaction, as a supplier or customer of the company, or even as a family member of a person having business or employment relationships with the company. These kinds of conflicts can often be addressed through disclosure of the conflict to the rest of the board followed by special care to isolate the director from the decision-making process and sensitive information related to the matter. It is more difficult to address the fundamental conflicts that arise when a director also serves as an employee, director, consultant, or advisor of a competitor. If the competition between the two companies is meaningful (not de minimus), ending the conflict may be necessary. Even aside from antitrust concerns, the director may need to either end the relationship with the competitor or step down from the board since there is no way to 'serve two masters.' Avoidance of these kinds of significant and on-going conflicts at the outset is important, and that is why companies often set forth in a code of conduct or board policy the requirement that directors not enter into relationships with competitors of the company." (Holly J. Gregory)

OECD Principle VI.B: Where board decisions may affect different shareholder groups differently, the board should treat all shareholders fairly.

> ➤ *In carrying out its duties, the board should not be viewed, or act, as an assembly of individual representatives for various constituencies. While specific board members may be nominated or elected by certain shareholders (and sometimes contested by others) it is an important feature*

of the board's work that board members when
they assume their responsibilities carry out their
duties in an evenhanded manner regarding all
shareholders. This principle is important to estab-
lish in the presence of controlling shareholders
that de facto *may select all board members.*

Director responsibilities in state-owned enterprises:
"All directors have the same responsibilities and are
required to act in the best interests of the corporation.
The board is not a parliament comprised of directors
representing different interests. In a state-owned enterprise, the "best interests of the corporation" should
extend to any public interest the state is executing
through the state-owned enterprise." (Peter Dey)

"The state is different than other types of share-
holders because it has an interest other than a
return on shares. The state may have policy objec-
tives that it wishes to achieve through the vehicle of
a state-owned enterprise, for example, increasing
employment or locating businesses in undevel-
oped regions. State policy objectives should be
explicitly acknowledged in the boardroom, along
with the obligation of directors to meet those
policy objectives before pursuing profits This is
critical particularly where those policy objectives
are not consistent with profitability. This is prefer-
able to viewing the board as a political forum of
people representing different views, which could
result in investors discounting the shares because

of a lack of knowledge about the company's real objectives." (Jonathan Koppell)

Ownership responsibilities in state-owned enterprises:
"Each state should view its holdings in state-owned enterprises as investments rather than political tools. With ownership comes responsibility, and in many countries, central institutions with the competence to fulfil those responsibilities may need to be established." (Lars Johan Cederlund)

Privatization and the evolution of the board:
"Following privatization, companies may inherit blocks of shareholders with different backgrounds and interests (such as strategic operators, institutional investors, and financial investors.) This can lead to boards being populated by members who are driven by their own special interests rather than the best interests of the corporation; this is not a sustainable situation and may drive down the value of the company. Companies seeking to privatize should ensure that robust governance requirements are in place, for example, by including commitments on the part of each party that wishes to buy shares in the privatized company or through listing standards of the relevant exchange." - José Monforte

"In some countries, privatization of state-owned enterprises resulted in widely dispersed ownership structures, as shares in many companies were parceled out to citizens and/or employees. Over time, ownership became more consolidated as people sold their shares to entrepreneurs and investment funds. These shareholders began demanding representation on boards that were traditionally populated by friends of the CEO. Some CEOs resisted these efforts initially, preferring instead to rely on the support of employees (who were considered to be natural allies of the CEO.) This changed over time however, when CEOs realized the importance of investor support." - Leonardo Peklar

4. Ethical standards

OECD Principle VI.C: The board should apply high ethical standards. It should consider the interests of stakeholders.

The board has a key role in setting the ethical tone of a company, not only by its own actions, but also in appointing and overseeing key executives and the management in general. High ethical standards are in the long-term interests of the company to make it credible and trustworthy, not only in day-to-day operations but also regarding long-term commitments. To clarify the objectives of the board, many companies have found it useful to develop company codes of conduct based on professional standards and sometimes broader codes of behavior. The latter might include a voluntary commitment by the company (including its subsidiaries) to comply with the OECD Guidelines for Multinational Enterprises which reflect all four principles in the ILO Declaration on Fundamental Labor Rights.

"Tone at the top":

"Establishing a common operating philosophy of ethics and values in business, across cultures, geographies, and the business value-chain is one of the

toughest challenges for the board and top management. The board should begin by adopting a set of values to guide the functioning of the corporation, and articulating them throughout all levels of the organization, for example, through company-wide speeches by the CEO and/or directors, and company training programs. The message should be communicated strongly that decisions should be made in accordance with the value framework and that breaches will be penalized appropriately. Recruitment processes should focus on ensuring that employees embody the values of the company." (Dr. N. Balasubramanian)

"'Tone at the top' is like a tuning fork; values vibrate from top to bottom and from bottom to top within an organization. As part of its responsibility for the 'tone at the top,' the board should ask, 'What is the organization's pure note and when are people within the organization in tune?' The board should query where momentum is generated with respect to 'tone at the top,' who determines the values of the company, how those value systems are presented and received, and whether they form part of the company's policy governing its business dealings." (Dominique de La Garanderie)

Company-wide codes serve as a standard for conduct by both the board and key executives, setting the framework for exercising judgement in dealing with varying and often conflicting constituencies. At a minimum, the ethical code should set clear limits on pursuing private interests, including dealings in the shares of the company. An overall framework for ethical conduct goes beyond compliance with the law, which should always be a fundamental requirement.

Codes of conduct and ethics in international companies:
"International companies, particularly those operating in developing countries, should ensure that they have a code of ethics that is strictly enforced throughout all areas of the company. For example, if a company discovers that management of a subsidiary is engaged in unethical conduct (such as attempting to influence customers by providing extravagant gifts or paying salaries to people with relatives working to influence business), the company should take immediate action and fire people where required." (Jack Krol)

Board communication with employees:
"Site visits by the board and direct communication between directors and employees can be an effective way of driving a message home across an organization and ensuring that everyone is 'singing from the same hymn book.' For example, directors may wish to speak to employees about 'tone at the top' and issues the board is focused on as an oversight group, while emphasizing that the CEO is in charge as the manager of the company. Directors should ensure that they communicate confidence in the management team and avoid discussing management issues with employees to minimize the risk of mixed messages." (Jack Krol)

5. Corporate strategy, risk policy and performance objectives

OECD Principle VI.D.1: Reviewing and guiding corporate strategy, major plans of action, risk policy, annual budgets and business plans; setting performance objectives; monitoring implementation and corporate

performance; and overseeing major capital expenditures, acquisitions, and divestitures.

Strategic oversight:
"Strategy should be regarded as a fundamental board issue. The whole board should be involved in strategic development –the executive directors should have in-depth knowledge about the company's competitive position, while non-executive directors provide an outside perspective.

For example, an outside director once inquired as to the advantages and disadvantages of concentrating company resources on confectionery and drinks and selling the company's food business. To answer the question, management was required to determine what resources would be released by the sale of the food business and what options the company had available to it to utilize those resources. No decision was reached at the initial board meeting held to discuss the issue, but a decision was made thereafter to sell the food business and concentrate on the company's international brands. This was not an easy decision, particularly as the food business included Cadbury cocoa, one of the company's original products. However, as Sir John Harvey-Jones has said, the strategic move was required so as to 'create tomorrow's company out of today's.'" (Adrian Cadbury)

"Boards should be involved in strategic development and risk oversight. However, in some developing countries, the board's role in practice has been minimal and reactive. Instead, majority shareholders may consult with executives to set the strategic direction of the company and manage risk. Boards may become more active in strategic development, risk oversight, and setting the 'tone at the top' through use of the 'balanced scorecard' approach. The balanced scorecard is a technical approach that utilizes the expertise of board members by connecting the broad vision and strategic direction of the company to its operational targets and outcomes. Board involvement in strategy is useful in helping management bring the strategy down to the operating level. The board should discuss with management the types of reports management will submit to the board and become involved in operating plans and targets; such involvement enhances oversight by enabling the board to determine whether management is effectively executing the strategy." (Jesus Estanislao)

"The board may listen to presentations by outside advisors such as market researchers and consulting firms who can provide forecasts, analyses of trends, market forces and strengths/weaknesses, opportunities and threats facing the company, and alternative strategic options. These presentations may be preceded or followed by management presentations. The board can then debate strategic scenarios amongst themselves and with management and select a strategy. The board may request management to provide it with a risk profile relating to the selected strategy and will consider how to mitigate and manage key risks." (Charnchai Charuvastr)

"The role of the board is to approve overarching strategies of the company and to provide support to management in the execution of those strategies.

Independent directors in particular can provide a perspective to the discussion based on their experience, technical expertise, and wisdom that makes a great contribution in the area of strategy. Effective strategic oversight requires directors to be informed and engaged. Directors are required to know the basics of the company's business and must pay attention in the boardroom.

Directors should invest time to understand the industry in which the company operates, as well as how the company makes money, and should read information relating to competitors as well as industry reports prepared by analysts.

Management is responsible for initial strategic development and should present their primary and alternative strategies to the board along with their background material, competitive analysis, rationale, and reasoning. This material should be sent to the board in advance to allow directors time to digest and analyze it before meeting with management. The board should thoroughly test management on its assumptions and the details of the strategy by asking many questions and should send management back to the drawing board on issues if required. For example, at some strategy reviews, 70 percent of meeting time can be spent on questions, with management presentations occupying the remainder of the time. Strategy should be viewed as a living, breathing process and not as something the board focuses on once a year. An effective board should look at the strategic context for the board's discussions and decisions as the year progresses, regularly test assumptions underlying the strategy, and monitor continuously to ensure that the company is achieving what the board thought it would be achieving. The board has the right to challenge management if progress is not proceeding as planned. If the CEO misses plan after plan but maintains to the board that he or she can turn it around, the board should ask how the CEO will make it happen, agree on a timeframe for evaluation, and how the turnaround will be funded within the strategy."   (Michele Hooper)

Summary:

The *OECD Principles*, adopted in 1999 and expanded in 2004, describe the basic elements of an effective corporate governance framework for corporations that seek to attract capital from equity investors. It covers topics such as: It covers topics such as:

- Promoting transparent and efficient markets which follow the rule of law and which clearly articulate the division of responsibilities among supervisory, regulatory, and enforcement authorities
- Protecting and facilitating the exercise of shareholders' rights
- Ensuring the equitable treatment of all shareholders, who should also obtain effective redress for violation of their rights
- Recognizing the rights of stakeholders established by law or through mutual agreements and encouraging active cooperation between corporations and stakeholders in creating wealth,

jobs, and the sustainability of financially sound enterprises

* Ensuring that timely and accurate disclosure is made on all material matters regarding the corporation, including its financial situation, performance, ownership, and governance
* Ensuring the strategic guidance of the company, the effective monitoring of management by the board, and the board's accountability to the company and the shareholders

The Responsibilities of the Board

The corporate governance framework should ensure the strategic guidance of the company, the effective monitoring of management by the board, and the board's accountability to the company and the shareholders. Directors should act on an informed basis, in good faith, with due diligence and care, and in the best interest of the company and the shareholders.

a) Where board decisions may affect different shareholder groups differently, the board should treat all shareholders fairly.
b) The board should apply high ethical standards. It should consider the interests of stakeholders.
c) The board should fulfill certain key functions, including:

1. *Reviewing and guiding corporate strategy, major plans of action, risk policy, annual budgets, and business plans; setting performance objectives; monitoring implemen-*

tation and corporate performance; and over-seeing major capital expenditures, acquisitions, and divestitures.

2. *Monitoring the effectiveness of the company's governance practices and making changes as needed.*

3. *Selecting, compensating, monitoring and, when necessary, replacing key executives and overseeing succession planning.*

4. *Aligning key executive and board remuneration with the longer-term interests of the company and its shareholders.*

5. *Ensuring a formal and transparent board nomination and election process.*

6. *Monitoring and managing potential conflicts of interest within management, directors, and shareholders, including misuse of corporate assets and abuse in related party transactions.*

7. *Ensuring the integrity of the corporation's accounting and financial reporting systems, including the independent audit, and seeing that systems of control are in place, systems for risk management, financial and operational control, and compliance with the law and relevant standards.*

d) The board should be able to exercise objective independent judgement on corporate affairs.

1. *Boards should assign enough nonexecutive directors capable of exercising independent judgement to tasks where there is a potential*

for conflict of interest. Examples of such key responsibilities are ensuring the integrity of financial and non-financial reporting, the review of related party transactions, nomination of directors and key executives, and board remuneration.

2. *When committees of the board are established, their mandate, composition, and working procedures should be well defined and disclosed by the board.*

3. *Directors should be able to commit them selves effectively to their responsibilities.*

To fulfil their responsibilities, directors should have access to accurate, relevant and timely information.

The Responsibilities of the Boards of State-Owned Enterprises

The boards of state-owned enterprises should have the authority, competencies, and objectivity to carry out their function of strategic guidance and monitoring of management. They should act with integrity and be held accountable for their actions.

a) The boards of SOEs should be assigned a clear mandate and the ultimate responsibility for the company's performance. The board should be accountable to the owners, act in the best interest of the company, and treat all shareholders equitably.

b) SOE boards should carry out their functions of monitoring of management and strategic guidance, subject to the objectives set by the government and the ownership entity. They should have the power to appoint and remove the CEO.

c) The boards of SOEs should be composed so that they can exercise objective and independent judgement. Good practice calls for the Chair to be separate from the CEO.

d) If employee representation on the board is mandated, mechanisms should be developed to guarantee this representation is exercised effectively and contributes to the enhancement of the board skills, information, and independence.

e) When necessary, SOE boards should set up specialized committees to support the full board in performing its functions, particularly regarding audit, risk management, and remuneration.

f) SOE boards should carry out an annual evaluation to appraise their performance.

The OECD Principles of Corporate Governance

1. Ensuring the Basis for an Effective Corporate Governance Framework

The corporate governance framework should promote transparent and efficient markets, follow the rule of law, and clearly articulate the division of responsibilities among different supervisory, regulatory, and enforcement authorities.

a) The corporate governance framework should be developed with a view to its impact on overall economic performance, market integrity, and the incentives it creates for market participants.

b) The legal and regulatory requirements that affect corporate governance practices in a jurisdiction should follow the rule of law, being transparent and enforceable.

c) The division of responsibilities among different authorities in a jurisdiction should be articulated and ensure that the public interest is served.

d) Supervisory, regulatory, and enforcement authorities should have the authority, integrity, and resources to fulfil their duties in a professional and objective manner.

Their rulings should be timely, transparent, and fully explained.

2. The Rights of Shareholders and Key Ownership Functions

The corporate governance framework should protect and facilitate the exercise of shareholders' rights.

a) Basic shareholder rights should include the right to: 1) secure methods of ownership registration; 2) convey or transfer shares; 3) obtain relevant and material information on the corporation on a timely and regular basis; 4) participate and vote in general shareholder meetings; 5) elect and remove members of the board; and 6) share in the profits of the corporation.

b) Shareholders could participate in, and to be sufficiently informed on, decisions about fundamental corporate changes such as: 1) amendments to the statutes, or articles of incorporation or similar governing documents of the company; 2) the authorization of additional shares; and 3) extraordinary transactions, including the transfer of all or substantially all assets, that in effect result in the sale of the company.

c) Shareholders should participate effectively and vote in general shareholder meetings and should be informed of the rules, including voting procedures, that govern general shareholder meetings:

1. *Shareholders should be furnished with sufficient and timely information about the date, location and agenda of general meetings, and full and timely information regarding the issues to be decided at the meeting.*

2. *Shareholders should ask questions to the board, including questions relating to the annual external audit, to place items on the agenda of general meetings, and to propose resolutions, subject to reasonable limitations.*

3. *Effective shareholder participation in key corporate governance decisions, such as the nomination and election of board members, should be facilitated. Shareholders should be able to make their views known on the remuneration policy for board members and key executives. The equity component of*

compensation schemes for board members and employees should be subject to shareholder approval.

4. *Shareholders should be able to vote in person or in absentia, and equal effect should be given to votes whether cast in person or in absentia.*

d) Capital structures and arrangements that enable certain shareholders to obtain control disproportionate to their equity ownership should be disclosed.

e) Markets for corporate control should be allowed to function in an efficient and transparent manner.

1. *The rules and procedures governing the acquisition of corporate control in the capital markets, and extraordinary transactions such as mergers and sales of substantial portions of corporate assets, should be clearly articulated and disclosed so investors understand their rights and recourse. Transactions should occur at transparent prices and under fair conditions that protect the rights of all shareholders according to their class.*

2. *Anti-takeover devices should not be used to shield management and the board from accountability.*

f) The exercise of ownership rights by all shareholders, including institutional investors, should be facilitated.

1. *Institutional investors acting in a fiduciary capacity should disclose their overall corporate governance and voting policies regarding their investments, including the procedures they have in place for deciding on using their voting rights.*

2. *Institutional investors acting in a fiduciary capacity should disclose how they manage material conflicts of interest that may affect the exercise of key ownership rights regarding their investments.*

g) Shareholders, including institutional shareholders, should be allowed to consult with each other on issues about their basic shareholder rights as defined in the Principles, subject to exceptions to prevent abuse.

3. The Equitable Treatment of Shareholders

The corporate governance framework should ensure the equitable treatment of all shareholders, including minority and foreign shareholders. All shareholders should obtain effective redress for violation of their rights.

a) All shareholders of the same series of a class should be treated equally.

1. *Within any series of a class, all shares should carry the same rights.*

2. *All investors should be able to obtain information about the rights attached to all series and classes of shares before they purchase. Any changes in voting rights should be approved by those classes of shares negatively affected.*
3. *Minority shareholders should be protected from abusive actions by, or in the interest of, controlling shareholders acting either directly or indirectly, and should have effective means of redress.*
4. *Votes should be cast by custodians or nominees in a manner agreed upon with the beneficial owner of the shares.*
5. *Impediments to cross border voting should be eliminated.*
6. *Processes and procedures for general shareholder meetings should allow for equitable treatment of all shareholders. Company procedures should not make it unduly difficult or expensive to cast votes.*

a) Insider trading and abusive self-dealing should be prohibited.
b) Members of the board and key executives should have to disclose to the board whether they, directly, indirectly or on behalf of third parties, have a material interest in any transaction or matter directly affecting the corporation.

4. The Role of Stakeholders in Corporate Governance

The corporate governance framework should recognize the rights of stakeholders established by law or through mutual agreements and encourage active cooperation between corporations and stakeholders in creating wealth, jobs, and the sustainability of financially sound enterprises.

a) The rights of stakeholders established by law or through mutual agreements are to be respected.

b) Where stakeholder interests are protected by law, stakeholders should obtain effective redress for violation of their rights.

c) Performance-enhancing mechanisms for employee participation should be permitted to develop.

d) Where stakeholders participate in the corporate governance process, they should have access to relevant, sufficient, and reliable information on a timely and regular basis.

e) Stakeholders, including individual employees and their representative bodies, should be able to freely communicate their concerns about illegal or unethical practices to the board and their rights should not be compromised for doing this.

f) The corporate governance framework should be complemented by an effective, efficient insolvency framework and by effective enforcement of creditor rights.

5. Disclosure and Transparency

The corporate governance framework should ensure that timely and accurate disclosure is made on all material matters regarding the corporation, including the financial situation, performance, ownership, and governance of the company.

a) Disclosure should include, but not be limited to, material information on:

1. *The financial and operating results of the company.*
2. *Company objectives.*
3. *Major share ownership and voting rights.*
4. *Remuneration policy for members of the board and key executives, and information about board members, including their qualifications, the selection process, other company directorships, and whether they are regarded as independent by the board.*
5. *Related party transactions.*
6. *Foreseeable risk factors.*
7. *Issues regarding employees and other stakeholders.*
8. *Governance structures and policies, the content of any corporate governance code or policy, and the process by which it is implemented.*

b) Information should be prepared and disclosed under high quality standards of accounting and financial and non-financial disclosure.

c) An annual audit should be conducted by an independent, competent and qualified auditor to provide an external and objective assurance to the board and shareholders that the financial statements fairly represent the financial position and performance of the company materially.

d) External auditors should be accountable to the shareholders and owe a duty to the company to exercise due professional care in the conduct of the audit.

e) Channels for disseminating information should provide for equal, timely and cost-efficient access to information by users.

f) The corporate governance framework should be complemented by an effective approach that addresses and promotes the provision of analysis or advice by analysts, brokers, rating agencies and others, that relates to decisions by investors, free from material conflicts of interest that might compromise the integrity of their analysis or advice.

6. The Responsibilities of the Board

The corporate governance framework should ensure the strategic guidance of the company, the effective monitoring of management by the board, and the board's accountability to the company and the shareholders.

a) Board members should act on a fully informed basis, in good faith, with due diligence and care, and in the best interest of the company and the shareholders.

b) Where board decisions may affect different shareholder groups differently, the board should treat all shareholders fairly.

c) The board should apply high ethical standards. It should consider the interests of stakeholders.

d) The board should fulfil certain key functions, including:

1. *Reviewing and guiding corporate strategy, major plans of action, risk policy, annual budgets and business plans; setting performance objectives; monitoring implementation and corporate performance; and overseeing major capital expenditures, acquisitions, and divestitures.*

2. *Monitoring the effectiveness of the company's governance practices and making changes as needed.*

3. *Selecting, compensating, monitoring and, when necessary, replacing key executives and overseeing succession planning.*

4. *Aligning key executive and board remuneration with the longer-term interests of the company and its shareholders.*

5. *Ensuring a formal and transparent board nomination and election process.*

6. *Monitoring and managing potential conflicts of interest of management, board members and shareholders, including misuse of corporate assets and abuse in related party transactions.*

7. *Ensuring the integrity of the corporation's accounting and financial reporting systems, including the independent audit, and that appropriate systems of control are in place, in particular, systems for risk management, financial and operational control, and compliance with the law and relevant standards.*
8. *Overseeing the process of disclosure and communications.*

e) The board should be able to exercise objective independent judgement on corporate affairs.

1. *Boards should assign enough non-executive board members capable of exercising independent judgement to tasks where there is a potential for conflict of interest. Examples of such key responsibilities are ensuring the integrity of financial and non-financial reporting, the review of related party transactions, nomination of board members and key executives, and board remuneration.*
2. *When committees of the board are established, their mandate, composition and working procedures should be well defined and disclosed by the board.*
3. *Board members should be able to commit themselves effectively to their responsibilities.*

f) To fulfil their responsibilities, board members should have access to accurate, relevant, and timely information.

PART TWO
ANNOTATIONS TO THE OECD
PRINCIPLES OF CORPORATE
GOVERNANCE

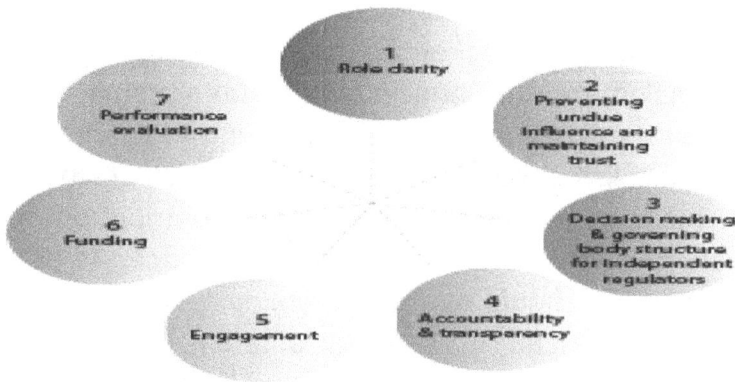

1
Role clarity

2
Preventing
undue
influence and
maintaining
trust

7
Performance
evaluation

6
Funding

3
Decision making
& governing
body structure
for independent
regulators

5
Engagement

4
Accountability
& transparency

1. Ensuring the Basis for an Effective Corporate Governance Framework

The corporate governance framework should promote transparent and efficient markets, follow the rule of law and clearly articulate the division of responsibilities among different supervisory, regulatory, and enforcement authorities.

To ensure an effective corporate governance framework, it is necessary that an appropriate and effective legal, regulatory, and institutional foundation is established upon which all market participants can rely on establishing their private contractual relations. This corporate governance framework typically comprises elements of legislation, regulation, self-regulatory arrangements, voluntary commitments, and business practices that result from a country's specific circumstances, history, and tradition. The desirable mix between legislation, regulation, self-regulation, voluntary standards, etc. in this area will, therefore, vary from country to country.

As new experiences accrue and business circumstances change, the content and structure of this framework might need to be adjusted. Countries seeking to implement the principles should monitor their corporate governance framework, including regulatory and listing requirements and business practices, to maintain and to strengthen its contribution to market integrity and economic performance. As part of this, they should take into account the interactions and complementarity between different elements of the corporate governance framework and its overall ability to promote ethical, responsible, and transparent corporate governance practices. Such analysis should be viewed as an important tool in developing an effective corporate governance framework. Effective and continuous consultation with the public is an essential element widely regarded as good practice. In developing a corporate governance framework in each jurisdiction, national legislators and regulators should duly consider the need for, and the results from, effective international dialogue and cooperation. If these conditions are met, the governance system is more likely to avoid over-regulation, support the exercise of entrepreneurship, and limit the risks of damaging conflicts of interest in both the private sector and in public institutions.

a) The corporate governance framework should be developed with a view to its impact on overall economic performance, market integrity, and the incentives it creates for market participants and the promotion of transparent and efficient markets.

The corporate form of organization of economic activity is a powerful force for growth. The regulatory and legal environment within which corporations operate is crucial to overall economic outcomes. Policymakers must put in place a framework that is flexible enough to meet the needs of corporations operating in widely different circumstances, facilitating their development of new opportunities to create value and to determine the most efficient deployment of resources. To achieve this goal, policymakers should remain focused on the ultimate economic outcomes, and when considering policy options, they will need to undertake an analysis of the impact on key variables that affect the functioning of markets, such as incentive structures, the efficiency of self-regulatory systems, and dealing with systemic conflicts of interest. Transparent and efficient markets discipline market participants and promote accountability.

b) The legal and regulatory requirements that affect corporate governance practices in a jurisdiction should follow the rule of law, transparent and enforceable.

If new laws and regulations are needed to deal with clear cases of market imperfections, they should be designed to make it possible to implement and enforce them in an efficient and even-handed manner covering all parties. Consultation by government and other regulatory authorities with corporations, their representative organizations, and other stakeholders is an effective way of doing this. Mechanisms should also be established for parties to protect their rights. To avoid over-regulation, unenforceable laws, and unintended consequences that may impede or distort business dynamics, policy measures should be designed with a view to their overall costs and benefits. Such assessments should consider the need for effective enforcement, including the ability of authorities to deter dishonest behavior and to impose effective sanctions for violations.

Corporate governance objectives are also formulated in voluntary codes and standards without the status of law or regulation. While such codes play an important role in improving corporate governance arrangements, they might leave shareholders and other stakeholders with uncertainty about their status and implementation. When codes and principles are a national standard or used as an explicit substitute for legal or regulatory provisions, market credibility requires that their status in terms of coverage, implementation, compliance, and sanctions is specified.

c) The division of responsibilities among different authorities in a jurisdiction should be clearly articulated and ensure that the public interest is served.

Corporate governance requirements and practices are typically influenced by an array of legal domains, such as company law, securities regulation, accounting and auditing standards, insolvency law, contract law, labor law, and tax law. Under these circumstances, there is a risk that the variety of legal influences may cause unintentional overlaps and even conflicts, which may frustrate the ability to pursue key corporate governance objectives. Policymakers should be aware of this risk and take measures to limit it. Effective enforcement also requires that the allocation of responsibilities for supervision, implementation, and enforcement among different authorities is defined, so the competencies of complementary bodies and agencies are respected and used most effectively. Overlapping and perhaps contradictory regulations between national jurisdictions is also an issue that should be monitored so that no regulatory vacuum may develop (i.e., issues slipping through in which no authority has explicit responsibility) and to minimize the cost of compliance with multiple systems by corporations. When regulatory responsibilities or oversight are delegated to non-public bodies, it is desirable to explicitly assess why, and under what circumstances, such delegation is desirable. It is also essential that the governance structure of any such delegated institution be transparent and encompasses the public interest.

d) Supervisory, regulatory, and enforcement authorities should have the authority, integrity, and resources to fulfill their duties in a professional and objective manner. Their rulings should be timely, transparent, and fully explained.

Regulatory responsibilities should be vested with bodies that can pursue their functions without conflicts of interest and that are subject to judicial review. As the number of public companies, corporate events, and the volume of disclosures increases, the resources of supervisory, regulatory, and enforcement authorities may come under strain. To follow developments, they will have a significant demand for fully qualified staff to provide effective oversight and investigative capacity - which will need to be appropriately funded. The ability to attract staff on competitive terms will enhance the quality and independence of supervision and enforcement.

2. The Rights of Shareholders and Key Ownership Functions

The corporate governance framework should protect and facilitate the exercise of shareholders' rights.

Equity investors have certain property rights. For example, an equity share in a publicly traded company can be bought, sold, or transferred. An equity share also entitles the investor to participate in the profits of the corporation, with liability limited to the investment. In addition, ownership of an equity share provides a right to information about the corporation and a right to influence the corporation, primarily by participation in general shareholder meetings and by voting.

As a practical matter, however, the corporation cannot be managed by shareholder referendum. The shareholding body comprises individuals and institutions whose interests, goals, investment horizons, and capabilities vary. The corporation's management must be able to make business decisions rapidly. Because of these realities and the complexity of managing the corporation's affairs in fast moving and ever-changing markets, shareholders are not expected to assume responsibility for managing corporate activities. The responsibility for corporate strategy and operations is typically placed in the hands of the board and a management team selected, motivated, and, when necessary, replaced by the board. Shareholders' rights to influence the corporation center on certain fundamental issues, such as the election of board members or other means of influencing the composition of the board, amendments to the company's organic documents, approval of extraordinary transactions, and other basic issues as specified in company law and internal company statutes. This Section is a statement of the most basic rights of shareholders, which are recognized by law in virtually all OECD countries. Additional rights such as the approval or election of auditors, direct nomination of board members, the ability to pledge shares, approving distributions of profits, etc., can be found in various jurisdictions.

   a) Basic shareholder rights should include the right to: 1) secure methods of ownership registration; 2) convey or transfer shares; 3) obtain relevant and material information on the corporation on a timely and regular basis; 4) participate and vote in general shareholder meetings; 5) elect and remove members of the board; and 6) share in the profits of the corporation.
   b) Shareholders could participate in, and to be sufficiently informed on, decisions about fundamental corporate changes such as: 1) amendments to the statutes, or articles of incorporation or similar governing documents of the company; 2) the authorization of additional shares; and 3) extraordinary transactions, including the transfer of all or substantially all assets, that in effect results in the sale of the company.

The ability of companies to form partnerships and related companies and to transfer operational assets, cash flow rights, and other rights and obligations to them is important for business flexibility and for delegating accountability in complex organizations. It also allows a company to divest itself of operational assets and to become only a holding company. However, without appropriate checks and balances, such possibilities may also be abused.

c) Shareholders should participate effectively and vote in general shareholder meetings and should be informed of the rules, including voting procedures, that govern general shareholder meetings.

1. *Shareholders should be furnished with sufficient and timely information about the date, location and agenda of general meetings, and full and timely information regarding the issues to be decided at the meeting.*

2. *Shareholders should ask questions to the board, including questions relating to the annual external audit, to place items on the agenda of general meetings, and to propose resolutions, subject to reasonable limitations. To encourage shareholder participation in general meetings, some companies have improved the ability of shareholders to place items on the agenda by simplifying filing amendments and resolutions. Improvements have also been made to make it easier for shareholders to submit questions before the general meeting and to obtain replies from management and board members. Shareholders should also be able to ask questions relating to the external audit report. Companies are not justified in assuming that abuses of such opportunities do not occur. It is reasonable, for example, to require that for shareholder resolutions to be placed on the agenda, they need to be*

supported by shareholders holding a speci-
fied market value or percentage of shares or
voting rights. This threshold should be deter-
mined considering ownership concentration,
to ensure that minority shareholders are
not effectively prevented from putting any
items on the agenda. Shareholder resolu-
tions approved and falling within the compe-
tence of the shareholders' meeting should be
addressed by the board.

3. Effective shareholder participation in key corporate governance decisions, such as the nomination and election of board members, should be facilitated. Shareholders should be able to make their views known on the remuneration policy for board members and key executives. The equity component of compensation schemes for board members and employees should be subject to shareholder approval.

To elect the members of the board is a basic shareholder right. For the election process to be effective, shareholders should be able to participate in the nomination of board members and vote on individual nominees or on different lists of them. Shareholders have access in several countries to the company's proxy materials sent to shareholders, although sometimes subject to conditions to prevent abuse. Regarding nomination of candidates, boards in many companies have established nomination committees to ensure proper compliance with established nomination procedures and to facilitate and coordinate the search for a balanced and qualified board.

It is increasingly regarded as good practice in many countries for independent board members to have a key role on this committee. To further improve the selection process, the Principles also call for full disclosure of the experience and background of candidates for the board and the nomination process, which will allow an informed assessment of the abilities and suitability of each candidate.

The Principles call for the disclosing of remuneration policy by the board. It is important for shareholders to know the specific link between remuneration and company performance when they assess the capability of the board and the qualities they should seek in nominees for the board. Although board and executive contracts are not an appropriate subject for approval by the general meeting of shareholders, there should be a means by which they can express their views. Several countries have introduced an advisory vote which conveys the strength and tone of shareholder sentiment to the board without endangering employment contracts. With equity-based schemes, their potential to dilute shareholders' capital and to powerfully determine managerial incentives means they should be approved by shareholders, either for individuals or for the policy of the scheme. In an increasing number of jurisdictions, any material changes to existing schemes must also be approved.

4. Shareholders should be able to vote in person or in absentia, and equal effect should be given to votes – whether cast in person or in absentia.

The Principles recommend that voting by proxy be generally accepted. It is important to the promotion and protection of shareholder rights that investors can place reliance upon directed proxy voting. The corporate governance framework should ensure that proxies are voted under the direction of the proxy holder, and that disclosure is provided in relation to how undirected proxies will be voted. In those jurisdictions where companies may obtain proxies, it should be disclosed how the Chairperson of the meeting (as the usual recipient of shareholder proxies obtained by the company) will exercise the voting rights attached to undirected proxies. Where proxies are held by the board or management for company pension funds and for employee stock ownership plans, the directions for voting should be disclosed.

The objective of facilitating shareholder participation suggests that companies consider favorably the enlarged use of information technology in voting, including secure electronic voting in absentia.

a) **Capital structures and arrangements that enable certain shareholders to obtain a degree of control disproportionate to their equity ownership should be disclosed.**

Some capital structures allow a shareholder to exercise a degree of control over the corporation disproportionate to the shareholders' equity owner-ship in the company. Pyramid structures, cross share-holdings, and shares with limited or multiple voting rights can diminish the capability of non-controlling shareholders to influence corporate policy.

Besides ownership relations, other devices can affect control over the corporation. Shareholder agreements are a common means for groups of shareholders, who individually may hold relatively small shares of total equity, to act in concert to constitute an effective majority, or at least the largest single block of share-holders. Shareholder agreements usually give those participating in the agreements preferential rights to purchase shares if other parties to the agreement wish to sell. These agreements can also contain provisions that require those accepting the agreement not to sell their shares for a specified time. Shareholder agree-ments can cover issues such as how the board or the Chairman will be selected. The agreements can also oblige those in the agreement to vote as a block. Some countries have found it necessary to closely monitor such agreements and to limit their duration. Voting caps limit the number of votes that a shareholder may cast, regardless of the number of shares the share-holder may actually possess. Voting caps, therefore, redistribute control and may affect the incentives for shareholder participation in shareholder meetings.

Given the capacity of these mechanisms to redis-tribute the influence of shareholders on company policy, shareholders can reasonably expect that all such capital structures and arrangements be disclosed.

b) **Markets for corporate control should be allowed to function in an efficient and transparent manner.**

1. *The rules and procedures governing the acquisition of corporate control in the capital markets, and extraordinary transactions such as mergers and sales of substantial portions of corporate assets, should be clearly articulated and disclosed so investors understand their rights and recourse. Transactions should occur at transparent prices and under fair conditions that protect the rights of all shareholders according to their class.*
2. *Anti-takeover devices should not be used to shield management and the board from accountability.*

In some countries, companies employ anti-takeover devices. However, both investors and stock exchanges have complained about the possibility that widespread use of anti-takeover devices may be a serious impediment to the functioning of the market for corporate control. Sometimes, these defenses can simply be devices to shield the management or the board from shareholder monitoring. In implementing any anti-takeover devices and in dealing with takeover proposals, the fiduciary duty of the board to shareholders and the company must remain paramount.

c) **Exercising ownership rights by all shareholders, including institutional investors, should be facilitated.**

As investors may pursue different investment objectives, the Principles advocate no particular investment strategy and do not seek to prescribe the optimal investor activism. But in considering the costs and benefits of exercising their ownership rights, many investors are likely to conclude that positive financial returns and growth can be obtained by undertaking a reasonable amount of analysis and by using their rights.

1. *Institutional investors acting in a fiduciary capacity should disclose their overall corporate governance and voting policies regarding their investments, including the procedures they have in place for deciding on using their voting rights.*

It is increasingly common for shares to be held by institutional investors. The effectiveness and credibility of the entire corporate governance system and company oversight will, to a large extent, depend on institutional investors that can make informed use of their shareholder rights and effectively exercise their ownership functions in companies in which they invest. While this principle does not require institutional investors to vote their shares, it calls for disclosure of how they exercise their ownership rights with due consideration to cost effectiveness. For institutions acting in a fiduciary capacity, such as pension funds, collective investment schemes, and some activities of insurance companies, the right to vote can be considered part of the value of the investment being undertaken on behalf of their clients. Failure to exercise the ownership rights could cause a loss to the investor who should know the policy to be followed by the institutional investors.

In some countries, the demand for disclosure of corporate governance policies to the market is detailed and includes requirements for explicit strategies regarding the circumstances in which the institution will intervene in a company, the approach they will use for such intervention, and how they will assess the effectiveness of the strategy. In several countries institutional investors are either required to disclose their actual voting records or it is regarded as good practice and implemented on an "apply or explain" basis. Disclosure is either to their clients (only regarding the securities of each client) or with investment advisors to registered investment companies, which is a less costly procedure.

A complementary approach to participation in shareholders' meetings is to establish a continuing dialogue with portfolio companies. Such a dialogue between institutional investors and companies should be encouraged, especially by lifting unnecessary regulatory barriers, although it is incumbent on the company to treat all investors equally and not to divulge information (not currently provided to the market) to the institutional investors. The additional information provided by a company would normally include general background information about the markets in which the company is operating and further elaboration on information already available to the market. When fiduciary institutional investors have developed and disclosed a corporate governance policy, effective implementation requires that they also set aside the appropriate human and financial resources to pursue this policy so their beneficiaries and portfolio companies can expect to share in the benefits of its implementations.

2. *Institutional investors acting in a fiduciary capacity should disclose how they manage material conflicts of interest that may affect the exercise of key ownership rights regarding their investments.*

The incentives for intermediary owners to vote their shares and exercise key ownership functions may, under certain circumstances, differ from those of direct owners. Such differences may sometimes be commercially sound but may also arise from conflicts of interest, a particularly acute issue when the fiduciary institution is a subsidiary or an affiliate of another financial institution, especially an integrated financial group.

When such conflicts arise from material business relationships, for example, through an agreement to manage the portfolio company's funds, such conflicts should be identified and disclosed. Institutions should disclose what actions they are taking to minimize the potentially negative impact on their ability to exercise key ownership rights. Such actions may include the separation of bonuses for fund management from those related to acquiring new business elsewhere in the organization.

d) **Shareholders, including institutional shareholders, should be allowed to consult with each other on issues about their basic shareholder**

rights as defined in the Principles, subject to exceptions to prevent abuse.

It has long been recognized that in companies with dispersed ownership, individual shareholders might have too small a stake in the company to warrant the cost of making an investment in monitoring performance. If small shareholders did invest resources in such activities, others would also gain without having contributed (i.e. they are "free riders".) This effect, which lowers incentives for monitoring, is probably less of a problem for institutions, particularly financial institutions acting in a fiduciary capacity, in deciding whether to increase their ownership to a significant stake in individual companies, or to rather simply diversify. However, other costs associated with holding a significant stake might still be high. Often institutional investors are prevented from doing this because it is beyond their capacity or would require investing more of their assets in one company than may be prudent. To overcome this asymmetry which favors diversification, they should be allowed, and even encouraged, to cooperate and coordinate their actions in nominating and electing board members, placing proposals on the agenda, and holding discussions directly with a company to improve its corporate governance. More generally, shareholders should be allowed to communicate with each other without having to comply with the formalities of proxy solicitation.

It must be recognized, however, that cooperation among investors could also manipulate markets and obtain control over a company without being subject to any takeover regulations. Cooperation might also be used to circumvent competition law. In some countries, the ability of institutional investors to cooperate on their voting strategy is limited or prohibited. Shareholder agreements may also be closely monitored. However, if cooperation does not involve issues of corporate control, or conflict with concerns about market efficiency and fairness, the benefits of more effective ownership may still be obtained.

Necessary disclosure of cooperation among investors, institutional or otherwise, may have to come with provisions which prevent trading for a period to avoid the possibility of market manipulation.

5. The Equitable Treatment of Shareholders

The corporate governance framework should ensure the equitable treatment of all shareholders, including minority and foreign shareholders. All shareholders should obtain effective redress for violation of their rights.

Investors' confidence that the capital they provide will be protected from misuse or misappropriation by corporate managers, board members, or controlling shareholders is an important factor in the capital markets. Corporate boards, managers, and controlling shareholders may engage in activities that advance their own interests at the expense of non-controlling shareholders. In protecting investors, a distinction can usefully be made between *ex-ante* and *ex-post* shareholder rights. *Ex-ante* rights are, for example, preemptive rights and qualified majority requirements for certain decisions. *Ex-post* rights allow the seeking of redress once rights have been violated. In jurisdictions where the enforcement of the legal and regulatory framework is weak, some countries have found it desirable to strengthen the *ex-ante* rights of shareholders by means such as low share ownership thresholds for placing items on the agenda of the shareholders meeting or by requiring a supermajority of shareholders for certain important decisions. The Principles support equal treatment for foreign and domestic shareholders in corporate governance. They do not address government policies to regulate foreign direct investment.

One way that shareholders can enforce their rights is to initiate legal and administrative proceedings against management and board members. Experience has shown that an important determinant of how much shareholder rights are protected is whether effective methods exist to obtain redress for grievances at a reasonable cost and without excessive delay. The confidence of minority investors is enhanced when the legal system provides mechanisms for minority shareholders to sue when they have reasonable grounds to believe that their rights have been violated. The provision of such enforcement mechanisms is a key responsibility of legislators and regulators.

There is some risk that a legal system which enables any investor to challenge corporate activity in the courts can become prone to excessive litigation. Thus, many legal systems have introduced provisions to protect management and board members against litigation abuse via tests for the sufficiency of shareholder complaints, so-called safe harbors for management and board member actions (such as the business judgement rule) and safe harbors for disclosing information. A balance must be struck between allowing investors to seek remedies for infringement of ownership rights and avoiding excessive litigation. Many countries have found that alternative adjudication procedures, such as administrative hearings or arbitration procedures organized by the securities regulators or other regulatory bodies, are an efficient method for dispute settlement, at least at the first instance level.

b.*All shareholders of the same series of a class should be treated equally. Within any series of a class, all shares should carry the same rights. All investors should be able to obtain information about the rights attached to all series and classes of shares before they purchase. Any changes in voting rights should be approved by those classes of shares negatively affected.*

The optimal capital structure of the firm is best decided by the management and the board, subject to approval by the shareholders. Some companies issue preferred (or preference) shares which have a preference regarding receipt of the profits of the firm, but which normally have no voting rights. Companies may also issue participation certificates or shares without voting rights, which would presumably trade at different prices than shares with voting rights. These structures may be effective in distributing risk and reward in ways thought to be in the best interests of the company and to cost-efficient financing.

The Principles do not take a position on the concept of "one share, one vote." However, many institutional investors and shareholder associations support this concept. Investors can expect to be informed regarding their voting rights before they invest. Once they have invested, their rights should not be changed unless those holding voting shares could have participated in the decision. Proposals to change the voting rights of different series and classes of shares should be submitted for approval at general shareholders meetings by a specified majority of voting shares in the affected categories.

6. Minority shareholders should be protected from abusive actions by, or in the interest of, controlling shareholders acting either directly or indirectly, and should have effective means of redress.

Many publicly traded companies have a large controlling shareholder. While the presence of a controlling shareholder can reduce the agency problem by closer monitoring of management, weaknesses in the legal and regulatory framework may lead to the abuse of other shareholders in the company. The potential for abuse is marked where the legal system allows, and the market accepts, controlling shareholders to exercise a level of control which does not correspond to the level of risk they assume as owners, through exploiting legal devices to separate ownership from control, such as pyramid structures or multiple voting rights. Such abuse may be carried out in various ways, including the extraction of direct private benefits via high pay and bonuses for employed family members and associates, inappropriate related party transactions, systematic bias in business decisions, and changes in the capital structure through special issuance of shares favoring the controlling shareholder.

Besides disclosure, a key to protecting minority shareholders is a clearly articulated duty of loyalty by board members to the company and to all shareholders. Abuse of minority shareholders is most pronounced in those countries where the legal and regulatory framework is weak. A particular issue arises in some jurisdictions where groups of companies are prevalent and where the duty of loyalty of a board member might be ambiguous. In these cases, some countries are now moving to control negative effects by specifying that a transaction for another group company must be offset by receiving a corresponding benefit from other companies of the group. Other common provisions to protect minority shareholders, which have proven effective, include preemptive rights in relation to share issues, qualified majorities for certain shareholder decisions, and the possibility to use cumulative voting in electing members of the board. Under certain circumstances, some jurisdictions require or permit controlling shareholders to buy-out the remaining shareholders at a share price that is established through an independent appraisal. This is important when controlling shareholders decide to de-list an enterprise. Other means of improving minority shareholder rights include derivative and class action lawsuits. With the common aim of improving market credibility, the choice and ultimate design of different provisions to protect minority shareholders depends on the overall regulatory framework and the national legal system.

7. Votes should be cast by custodians or nominees in a manner agreed upon with the beneficial owner of the shares.

In some OECD countries it was customary for financial institutions which held shares in custody for investors to cast the votes of those shares. Custodians such as banks and brokerage firms holding securities as nominees for customers were sometimes required to vote supporting management unless specifically instructed by the shareholder to do otherwise.

The trend in OECD countries is to remove provisions that automatically enable custodian institutions to cast the votes of shareholders. Rules in some countries have recently been revised to require custodian institutions to provide shareholders with information about their options in using their voting rights. Shareholders may elect to delegate all voting rights to custodians. Shareholders may be informed of all upcoming shareholder votes and may cast some votes while delegating some voting rights to the custodian. It is necessary to draw a reasonable balance between assuring that shareholder votes are not cast by custodians without regard for the wishes of shareholders and not imposing excessive burdens on custodians to secure shareholder approval before casting votes. For example, if no instruction to the contrary is received, the custodian may vote the shares in the way it deems consistent with shareholder interest. This principle does not apply to exercising voting rights by trustees or other persons acting under a special legal mandate (such as bankruptcy receivers and estate executors.)

Holders of depository receipts should be provided with the same ultimate rights and practical opportunities to participate in corporate governance as accorded to holders of the underlying shares. Where the direct holders of shares may use proxies, the depositary, trust office, or equivalent body should issue proxies timely to depository receipt holders. The depository receipt holders should be able to issue binding voting instructions regarding the shares, which the depositary or trust office holds on their behalf.

8. Impediments to cross-border voting should be eliminated.

Foreign investors often hold their shares through chains of intermediaries. Shares are typically held in accounts with securities intermediaries that hold accounts with other intermediaries and central securities depositories in other jurisdictions, while the listed company resides in a third country.

Such cross-border chains cause special challenges regarding determining the entitlement of foreign investors to use their voting rights, and the means of communicating with such investors. Combined with business practices which provide only a short notice period, shareholders are often left with only very limited time to react to a convening notice by the

company and to make informed decisions about items
for decision. This makes cross-border voting difficult.
The legal and regulatory framework should clarify who
may control the voting rights in cross-border situations
and where to simplify the depository chain. Notice
periods should ensure that foreign investors in effect
have similar opportunities to exercise their ownership functions as domestic investors. To further facilitate voting by foreign investors, laws, regulations, and
corporate practices should allow participation through
means which make use of modern technology.

a) **Processes and procedures for general shareholder meetings should allow for equitable
treatment of all shareholders. Company procedures should not make it unduly difficult or
expensive to cast votes.**

The right to participate in general shareholder
meetings is a fundamental shareholder right.
Management and controlling investors have sought to
discourage non-controlling or foreign investors from
trying to influence the direction of the company. Some
companies have charged fees for voting. Other impediments included prohibitions on proxy voting and the
requirement of personal attendance at general shareholder meetings to vote. Still other procedures may
make it practically impossible to exercise ownership
rights. Proxy materials may be sent too close to the
time of general shareholder meetings to allow investors
adequate time for reflection and consultation. Many
companies in OECD countries are seeking to develop

better channels of communication and decision-making with shareholders. Efforts by companies to remove artificial barriers to participation in general meetings are encouraged and the corporate governance framework should facilitate the use of electronic voting in absentia.

b) Insider trading and abusive self-dealing should be prohibited.

Abusive self-dealing occurs when persons having close relationships to the company, including controlling shareholders, exploit those relationships to the detriment of the company and investors. As insider trading entails manipulation of the capital markets, it is prohibited by securities regulations, company law, and/ or criminal law in most OECD countries. However, not all jurisdictions prohibit such practices, and sometimes enforcement is not vigorous. These practices are breaching good corporate governance because they violate the principle of equitable treatment of shareholders.

The Principles reaffirm that it is reasonable for investors to expect that the abuse of insider power be prohibited. Where such abuses are not specifically forbidden by legislation, or where enforcement is not effective, it will be important for governments to take measures to remove any such gaps.

c) Members of the board and key executives should have to disclose to the board whether they directly, indirectly, or on behalf of third parties, have a material interest in any

transaction or matter directly affecting the corporation.

Members of the board and key executives have an obligation to inform the board when they have a business, family, or other special relationship outside of the company that could affect their judgement regarding a particular transaction or matter affecting the company. Such special relationships include situations where executives and board members have a relationship with the company via their association with a shareholder in a position to exercise control. Where a material interest has been declared, it is good practice for that person not to be involved in any decision involving the transaction or matter.

9. The Role of Stakeholders in Corporate Governance

The corporate governance framework should recognize the rights of stakeholders established by law or through mutual agreements and encourage active cooperation between corporations and stakeholders in creating wealth, jobs, and the sustainability of financially sound enterprises.

A key aspect of corporate governance is concerned with ensuring the flow of external capital to companies both in equity and credit. Corporate governance is also concerned with finding ways to encourage the stakeholders in the firm to undertake economically optimal levels of investment in firm-specific human and physical capital. The competitiveness and ultimate success of a corporation results from teamwork that embodies contributions from a range of different resource providers including investors, employees, creditors, and suppliers.

Corporations should recognize that the contributions of stakeholders constitute a valuable resource for building competitive and profitable companies. It is in the long-term interest of corporations to foster wealth-creating cooperation among stakeholders. The governance framework should recognize that the interests of the corporation are served by recognizing the interests of stakeholders and their contribution to the long-term success of the corporation.

a) **The rights of stakeholders established by law or through mutual agreements are to be respected.**

In all OECD countries, the rights of stakeholders are established by law (e.g., labor, business, and commercial and insolvency laws) or by contractual relations. Even in areas where stakeholder interests are not legislated, many firms commit to stakeholders, and concern over corporate reputation and corporate performance often requires the recognition of broader interests.

b) **Where stakeholder interests are protected by law, stakeholders should obtain effective redress for violation of their rights.**

The legal framework and process should be transparent and not impede the ability of stakeholders to communicate and to obtain redress for violating rights.

c) **Performance-enhancing mechanisms for employee participation should be permitted to develop.**

How much employees participate in corporate governance depends on national laws and practices and may vary from company to company. In corporate governance, performance- enhancing mechanisms for participation may benefit companies directly and indirectly through the readiness of employees to invest in firm-specific skills. One example of a mechanism for employee participation is employee representation on boards and governance processes, such as works councils that consider employee viewpoints in certain key decisions. Regarding performance-enhancing mechanisms, employee stock ownership plans or other profit-sharing mechanisms are in many countries. Pension commitments are also often an element of the relationship between the company and its past and present employees. Where such commitments involve establishing an independent fund, its trustees should be independent of the company's management and manage the fund for all beneficiaries.

d) **Where stakeholders participate in the corporate governance process, they should have access to relevant, sufficient, and reliable information on a timely and regular basis.**

Where laws and practice of corporate governance systems provide for participation by stakeholders, stakeholders should have access to information to fulfil their responsibilities.

e) **Stakeholders, including individual employees and their representative bodies, should be able to freely communicate their concerns about illegal or unethical practices to the board and their rights should not be compromised for doing this.**

Unethical and illegal practices by corporate officers may not only violate the rights of stakeholders but also be to the detriment of the company and its shareholders in terms of reputation effects and an increasing risk of future financial liabilities. It is to the advantage of the company and its shareholders to establish procedures and safe harbors for complaints by employees, either personally through their representative bodies, or via others outside the company, about illegal and unethical behavior. In many countries the board is being encouraged by laws and/or principles to protect these individuals and representative bodies, and to give them confidential direct access to someone independent on the board, often a member of an audit or an ethics committee. Some companies have established an ombudsman to deal with complaints. Several regulators have also established confidential phone and e-mail facilities to receive allegations. While in certain countries representative employee bodies undertake the tasks of conveying concerns to the company, individual employees should not be precluded from, or be less protected, when acting alone. When there is an inadequate response to a complaint regarding contravention of the law, the *OECD Guidelines for Multinational Enterprises* encourage them to report their *bona fide* complaint to the competent public authorities. The company should refrain from discriminatory or disciplinary actions against such employees or bodies.

f) **The corporate governance framework should be complemented by an effective, efficient insolvency framework and by effective enforcement of creditor rights.**

Especially in emerging markets, creditors are a key stakeholder and the terms, volume, and type of credit extended to firms will depend importantly on their rights and on their enforceability. Companies with a good corporate governance record can often borrow larger sums and on more favorable terms than those with poor records or which operate in nontransparent markets. The framework for corporate insolvency varies widely across countries. In some countries, when companies are nearing insolvency, the legislative framework imposes a duty on directors to act in the interests of creditors who might play a prominent role in the governance of the company. Other countries have mechanisms which encourage the debtor to reveal timely information about the company's difficulties so a consensual solution can be found between the debtor and its creditors.

Creditor rights vary, ranging from secured bond holders to unsecured creditors. Insolvency procedures usually require efficient mechanisms for reconciling the interests of different classes of creditors. In many jurisdictions provision is made for special rights such as through "debtor in possession" financing which provides incentives/protection for new funds provided to the enterprise in bankruptcy.

10. Disclosure and Transparency

The corporate governance framework should ensure that timely and accurate disclosure is made on all material matters regarding the corporation, including the financial situation, performance, ownership, and governance of the company.

In most OECD countries much information, both mandatory and voluntary, is compiled on publicly traded and large, unlisted enterprises, and disseminated to a broad range of users. Public disclosure is typically required, at a minimum, annually, though some countries require periodic disclosure on a semi-annual or quarterly basis, or even more frequently with material developments affecting the company. Companies often make voluntary disclosure that goes beyond minimum disclosure requirements in response to market demand. A strong disclosure regime that promotes real transparency is a pivotal feature of market-based monitoring of companies and is central to shareholders' ability to exercise their ownership rights on an informed basis.

Experience in countries with large and active equity markets shows that disclosure can also be a powerful tool for influencing the behavior of companies and for protecting investors. A strong disclosure regime can help to attract capital and maintain confidence in the capital markets. Weak disclosure and non-transparent practices can contribute to unethical behavior and to losing market integrity, at costs - not just to the company and its shareholders, but also to the economy. Shareholders and potential investors require access to regular, reliable, and comparable information in sufficient detail for them to assess the stewardship of management, and make informed decisions about the valuation, ownership, and voting of shares. Insufficient or unclear information may hamper the ability of the markets to function, increase the cost of capital, and result in a poor allocation of resources. Disclosure also helps improve public understanding of the structure and activities of enterprises, corporate policies and perfor- mance regarding environmental and ethical standards, and companies' relationships with the communities in which they operate.

11. The OECD Guidelines for Multinational Enterprises

Disclosure requirements are not expected to place unreasonable administrative or cost burdens on enter- prises. Nor are companies expected to disclose informa- tion that may endanger their competitive position unless disclosure is necessary to fully inform the investment decision-makers and to avoid misleading the investor. To determine what information should be disclosed at a minimum, many countries apply the concept of materi- ality. Material information can be defined as informa- tion whose omission or misstatement could influence the economic decisions taken by users of information. The Principles support timely disclosure of all material developments that arise between regular reports. They also support simultaneous reporting of information to all shareholders to ensure their equitable treatment. In maintaining close relations with investors and market participants, companies must be careful not to violate this fundamental principle of equitable treatment.

12.Disclosure should include, but not be limited to, material information on the financial and operating results of the company.

Audited financial statements showing the financial performance and the financial situation of the company (most typically including the balance sheet, the profit and loss statement, the cash flow statement, and notes to the financial statements) are the most widely used source of information on companies. In their current form, the two principal goals of financial statements are to enable appropriate monitoring to take place and to provide the basis to value securities. Management's discussion and analysis of operations is typically included in annual reports. This discussion is most useful when read with the financial statements. Investors are interested in information that may shed light on the future performance of the enterprise.

Arguably, failures of governance can often be linked to failing to disclose the "whole picture", particularly where off-balance-sheet items are used to provide guarantees or similar commitments between related companies. Transactions that relate to an entire group of companies should be disclosed in line with high quality internationally recognized standards and include information about contingent liabilities, off-balance-sheet transactions, and special purpose entities.

13. Company objectives.

Besides their commercial objectives, companies are encouraged to disclose policies relating to business ethics, the environment, and other public policy commitments. Such information may be important for investors and other users of information to better evaluate the relationship between companies and the communities in which they operate and the steps that companies have taken to implement their objectives.

14. Major share ownership and voting rights.

One of the basic rights of investors is to be informed about the ownership structure of the enterprise and their rights vis-à-vis the rights of other owners. The right to such information should also extend to information about the structure of a group of companies and intra-group relations. Such disclosures should make transparent the objectives, nature, and structure of the group. Countries often require disclosure of ownership data once certain thresholds of ownership are passed. Such disclosure might include data on major shareholders and others that, directly or indirectly, control or may control the company through special voting rights, shareholder agreements, the ownership of controlling or large blocks of shares, significant cross shareholding relationships, and cross guarantees.

Particularly for enforcement, and to identify potential conflicts of interest, related party transactions, and insider trading, information about record ownership may have to be complemented with information about beneficial ownership. Where major shareholdings are held through intermediary structures or arrangements, information about the beneficial owners should be obtainable at least by regulatory and enforcement agencies and/or through the judicial process. The OECD template *Options for Obtaining Beneficial Ownership and Control Information* can serve as a useful self-assessment tool for countries that wish to ensure necessary access to information about beneficial ownership.

15. Remuneration policy for members of the board and key executives, and information about board members, including their qualifications, the selection process, other company directorships, and whether they are regarded as independent by the board.

Investors require information on individual board members and key executives to evaluate their experience and qualifications and assess any potential conflicts of interest that might affect their judgement. For board members, the information should include their qualifications, share ownership in the company, membership on other boards and whether the board considers them an independent member. Disclosure of membership on other boards is important, not only because it is an indication of experience and possible time pressures facing a member of the board, but also because it may reveal potential conflicts of interest and makes transparent the degree to which there are interlocking boards.

Several national principles, and sometimes laws, lay down specific duties for board members who can be regarded as independent, and sometimes recommend that most of the board should be independent. In many countries, it is incumbent on the board to set out the reasons a member of the board can be considered independent. It is then up to the shareholders, and ultimately the market, to determine if those reasons are justified. Several countries have concluded that companies should disclose the selection process and especially whether it was open to a broad field of candidates. Such information should be provided before any decision by the general shareholder's meeting or on a continuing basis if the situation has changed materially.

Information about board and executive remuneration is also of concern to shareholders. Of particular interest is the link between remuneration and company performance. Companies are generally expected to disclose information on the remuneration of board members and key executives so investors can assess the costs and benefits of remuneration plans and the contribution of incentive schemes, such as stock option schemes, to company performance. Disclosure individually (including termination and retirement provisions) is increasingly regarded as good practice and is now mandated in several countries. In these cases, some jurisdictions call for remuneration of some the highest-paid executives to be disclosed, while in others it is confined to specified positions.

NOTE:

An effective corporate governance system, within an individual company and across an economy as a whole, helps to provide the confidence necessary for the proper functioning of a market economy. The cost of capital is lower, and firms are encouraged to use resources more efficiently, underpinning growth. Corporate governance is only part of the larger economic context in which firms operate that includes, for example, macroeconomic policies and competition in product and factor markets. The corporate governance framework also depends on the legal, regulatory, and institutional environment. In addition, factors such as business ethics and corporate awareness of the environmental and societal interests of the communities in which a company operates can also affect its reputation and its long-term success. While a multiplicity of factors affects the governance and decision-making processes of firms, and are important to their long-term success, the Principles focus on governance problems that result from the separation of ownership and control.

However, this is not simply an issue of the relationship between shareholders and management, although that is the central element. In some jurisdictions, governance issues also arise from the power of certain controlling shareholders over minority shareholders. In other countries, employees have important legal rights despite their ownership rights. The principles have to be complementary to a broader approach to operating checks and balances. Some of the other issues relevant to a company's decision-making processes, such as environmental, anti-corruption, or ethical concerns are considered but are treated more explicitly in several other OECD instruments (including the *Guidelines for Multinational Enterprises* and the *Convention on Combating Bribery of Foreign Public Officials in International Transactions),* as well as the instruments of other international organizations.

Corporate governance is affected by the relationships among participants in the governance system. Controlling shareholders, which may be individuals, family holdings, bloc alliances, or other corporations acting through a holding company or cross- shareholdings, can influence corporate behavior. As owners of equity, institutional investors are increasingly demanding a voice in corporate governance in some markets. Individual shareholders rarely seek to exercise governance rights but may be extremely concerned about obtaining fair treatment from controlling shareholders and management. Creditors play an important role in several governance systems and can serve as external monitors over corporate performance. Employees and other stakeholders play an important role in contributing to the long-term success and performance of the corporation, while governments establish the overall institutional and legal framework for corporate governance. The role of each participant and their interactions vary widely among OECD countries and among non-OECD countries. These relationships are subject to law and regulation and, in part, to voluntary adaptation and, most importantly, to market forces. How much corporations observe basic principles of good corporate governance is an increasingly important factor for investment decisions. Of particular relevance is the relation between corporate governance practices and the increasingly international character of investment. International flows of capital enable companies to access financing from a much larger pool of investors. If countries are to reap the full benefits of the global capital market, and if they are to attract long-term "patient" capital, corporate governance arrangements must be credible, well understood across borders, and adherence to internationally accepted principles.

Even if corporations do not rely primarily on foreign sources of capital, adherence to good corporate governance practices will help improve the confidence of domestic investors, reduce the cost of capital, underpin the good functioning of financial markets, and ultimately induce more stable sources of financing. There is no single model of good corporate governance. However, work carried out in both OECD and non-OECD countries and within the Organization has identified common elements that underlie good corporate governance. The Principles build on these common elements and are formulated to embrace the different models that exist. For example, they advocate no particular board structure and the term "board" as used in this document embraces the different national models of board structures found in OECD and non-OECD countries. In the typical two-tier system, found in some countries, "board" as used in the Principles refers to the "supervisory board" while "key executives" refers to the "management board." In systems where the unitary board is overseen by an internal auditor's body, the principles applicable to the board are also, *mutatis mutandis*, applicable. The terms "corporation" and "company" are used interchangeably in the text.

The Principles are non-binding and do not aim at detailed prescriptions for national legislation. Rather, they seek to identify objectives and suggest various means for achieving them. Their purpose is to serve as a reference point. They can be used by policy makers as they examine and develop the legal and regulatory frameworks for corporate governance that reflect their own economic, social, legal and cultural circumstances, and by market participants as they develop their own practices. The Principles are evolutionary and should be reviewed, given significant changes in circum-stances. To remain competitive in a changing world, corporations must innovate and adapt their corporate governance practices so they can meet new demands and grasp new opportunities. Similarly, governments must shape an effective regulatory framework that provides for sufficient flexibility to allow markets to function effectively and to respond to expectations of shareholders and other stakeholders. It is up to govern-ments and market participants to decide how to apply these Principles in developing their own frameworks for corporate governance, considering the costs and benefits of regulation.

The following document is divided into two parts. The principles in the first part of the document cover these areas:

(i) Ensuring the basis for an effective corporate governance framework.
(ii) The rights of shareholders and key ownership functions.
(iii) The equitable treatment of shareholders.
(iv) The role of stakeholders.
(v) Disclosure and transparency; and
(vi) The responsibilities of the board.

Each section is headed by a single Principle that appears in bold italics and is followed by several supporting sub-principles. In the second part of the document, the Principles are supplemented by annotations that contain commentary on the Principles and should help readers understand their rationale.

The annotations may also contain descriptions of dominant trends and offer alternative implementation methods and examples that may be useful in making the principles operational.

CONCLUSION

Far from being a "victimless crime," corruption infringes the fundamental human right to fair treatment. All persons should be treated equally, but when one person bribes a public official, he acquires a privileged status in relation to others. He becomes an "insider" while others are made "outsiders" (and the more "outside" they are, the extremely poor, the landless, women, ethnic minorities, the more they will be hurt.) Clare Short, the UK Secretary of State for International Development, notes a report in the Indian magazine Outlook to the effect that the bribe for a new water connection was 1,000 R. This effectively excluded the poor from access to running water, with all the health and time-loss implications this entails. Corruption is thus profoundly inegalitarian in its effects, having a "Robin Hood-in-reverse" characteristic. Hugh Bayley, MP, introducing a bill to combat offenses of international bribery and corruption, said that "bribery is a direct transfer of money from the poor to the rich."

The ramifications spread yet further. Productive foreign investment may be lost. Before the Asian crisis of 1997/98 there were some who argued that corruption was not harmful, it merely greased the wheels of commerce. Some pointed out that certain countries which ranked high in surveys of the level of corruption also excelled in economic growth. The World Development Report notes that the question of predictability (the amount to be paid, the certainty of outcome) throws some light on this apparent paradox. "For a given level of corruption, countries with more predictable corruption have higher investment rates…"

However, the Report stated that even in these countries' corruption hurt economic performance, because the higher transaction costs and increased uncertainty put off potential investors. Time magazine quotes research by Professor Shang-Jin Wei of Harvard School of Government to the effect that the high level of corruption in Mexico compared with Singapore was the equivalent of a 24 per cent increase in the marginal rate of taxation.

A conservationist, Lansen Olsen, in a letter to the Transparency International Newsletter notes that "political corruption is a major feature of the political habitat in which wildlife conservation efforts sink or swim." When corruption breaches regulations designed to protect the environment, everyone suffers in the long term, as losing primary forest leads to soil erosion, local climate change, etc., but the poor have the smallest resources with which to weather environmental degradation.

Corruption can also have ugly and unpredictable consequences for the (Western) briber. As soon as he pays, he loses control. If he does not get what he paid for he is in no position to complain. Having broken the law, he is vulnerable to blackmail. If he tries to break the corrupt relationship, he may face a variety of threats, including the threat of violence.

www.ingramcontent.com/pod-product-compliance
Lightning Source LLC
Chambersburg PA
CBHW061241220326
41599CB00028B/5496